BUTTER IN THE MORNING

Butter in the Morning

Georgia Green Stamper

WIND PUBLICATIONS

International Standard Book Number 978-1-936138-54-8
Library of Congress Control Number 2012952976

First edition

Cover photograph © Frank Anderson, *Lexington Herald-Leader*
Front cover design by Larry Treadway
Author photograph by Ernie Stamper

To the children

Shannan, Rebecca, and Georgia Ann

and to theirs

Jared, Eliza, Owen, Annelise, Hudson and Georgia Jane

Contents

To Every Thing There Is A Season

Butter In The Morning

Introduction

My little stories, though often connected by a Kentucky landscape and recurring characters, were written to stand alone. They emerged over a period of years, in different voices, sometimes laughing, sometimes not, and were scattered like breadcrumbs as I wandered deeper into the forest. When I followed them, however, intent on pressing them into books, I was surprised that all of them, even the lightest satires, led me home.

The essays in the first section "Where I'm From"—a title borrowed from George Ella Lyon's iconic poem—obviously spring from a particular geographic dot and a unique tribe of Kentucky country people. These stories were born in Owen County along the banks of Eagle Creek, and were shaped and nurtured by tobacco farmers.

Home, however, is more than time and place. It's more than faded images of people my mind hangs on to, unwilling to let them die, or the anecdotes snatched from their lives like snapshots and pasted into an album. It's all of these, but more. It's a clan's temperament and philosophy, its history and sense of humor, and it shows up throughout this collection of essays. "You Might As Well Laugh, Mother Always Said," and so we did, learning, like the ancient Greek dramatists, to use comedy to cut life down to a manageable size. Children of the soil, we heard the Preacher's words, "To Every Thing There is a Season," and we understood. The stories in the final, title section, "Butter in the Morning," wade in both deep and shallow waters, from reflections on racism to flooded basements, but each is shaped by my people's faith in perseverance. This, then, is the journal of

1

my quest to return home, like Dorothy, discovering what I carried in my heart all along.

Those who stumble upon *Butter in the Morning*, however, should be forewarned that I ramble over many subjects and leap through the nineteenth, twentieth, and twenty-first centuries in no chronological order whatsoever. Still, I believe the pieces create a pattern, like the fragments in the heirloom quilts hanging on the walls of my family room, and if read in order from the beginning to the end, become something large enough to wrap around my life.

I wrote some of the stories to hold them safe for my children and grandchildren and for my people who are not yet born. Others I wrote to figure out what I think about what I know and where I've been. Sometimes, I confess, I wrote because I needed to laugh or to grieve. But always I have written with the hope that my stories might help readers recover their own.

May you, too, remember, and find your way home.

Where I'm From

prologue i ...
where I'm from

I remember how the farm looked to me as I walked beside my grandfather along the deep-rutted dirt road on that autumn afternoon. More than anything else I felt the stillness of the day and of the place. Nothing seemed to move, not even the air, only me, as I leaped from the edge of one baked crater to another. The tracks had been cut in the prehistoric spring when the soft mud had reached up to pull the tractor and the cattle down into the earth itself. But now the ground lay hard and motionless. Even the bits of grass and weeds had dried into crisp stillness.

"Let's rest here," Gran Hudson said as he lowered himself to sit on a large rock jutting partway out of the ground in the shade of a walnut tree. He pointed toward the walnuts that had already been hulled by the tractor's passing, that laid exposed in the ruts, and that had dried enough in the hot sun to gather. "Pick us up some of those dry black ones, and we'll eat them."

Soon I found a dozen wrinkled little balls scattered in the lane that he deemed ready to eat. I piled them on the stone ledge, and sat down beside him with the walnuts between us. Gran picked up a small rock to use as a hammer, and began to smash the hard shells against the ledge where we sat. Then, with his Case pocketknife, he picked the nutmeat from the shattered shells, and dropped the morsels from his knife blade into my waiting palm. He began to talk then, to tell me the stories he'd told me before, about this place and about his people.

From where we sat under the walnut tree on top of the ridge, I could see down into the broad bottoms that stretched below us.

5

I wondered if I could walk until I reached Eagle Creek and its row of white, bony sycamore trees that reached from one far side of the valley on the left, to the other far side on the right. I wondered if I could walk from where I was, on top of the world, to the other side of the world, where the sky met the earth.

In the quiet, the sounds of the birds and insects and distant cattle melded into a single tone, a separate voice competing with Gran's for my attention. I closed my eyes and let the warm autumn sun swaddle me.

When I opened my eyes again, they rested on Gran and then on the wide valley that lay below us. Although I had not yet internalized all my grandfather's stories, I knew on some level where reason cannot reach that I belonged here.

At that moment, I knew that I was happy. I knew that this was what happiness was, to be at home with this place.

The Longest Creek in the World

It was one mile short of being a river, folks said when I was a child, and I believed them. Eagle Creek was our Nile, sustaining our livelihood, nurturing our culture. Its winding path had carved out our place on earth a million years before the mighty Ohio was born, mapping where the hearts of my people would rest. Even the edge of the sky stopped at a wall of tall, boney sycamore trees that grew along its banks.

On this side of Big Eagle lay my Gran Hudson's fine bottomland, the homeplace, where he and my parents and I lived together. On the other side lay 300 more acres, his too, but hillier, though still good enough tobacco land. We called that the farm across the creek.

Down the hill from our house, a dip and then a sharp turn beyond our view, an ancient covered bridge crossed Eagle Creek. Though the old bridge vanished in a dramatic nighttime fire when I was nine—replaced in time by a concrete span that stands today—I see my earliest memories filtered in the dim light of its tunnel. I hear Gran Hudson's voice under the muffled song of tires rolling over wooden treads worn slick and smooth with time. Crossing Eagle led to the rest of my known world. The Natlee covered bridge was its portal.

We had to cross Eagle Creek by way of the bridge to pick up a needed item at Tommy Reed's small Natlee store, a loaf of bread, a pound of coffee, or a cold Coca-Cola. We had to cross Eagle at the Natlee bridge to reach the village of New Columbus perched two hills beyond, where I learned Bible stories at the Methodist Church and how to read at the schoolhouse. From there, we would wind our way another five or six miles to the little town of Corinth, to its bank and the post office, the Grey-

7

hound bus station and the closest movie theater. But the road out also led us back home, across Eagle Creek again, and to bed.

Eagle could flood wild and wide in the early spring, and it frightened me then, its waters reaching places it should not be, like our tobacco fields or the flowered linoleum floors of Cousin Birdie True's living room. Then I would overhear my grandfather re-tell the old story about his grandfather, who was dumped into Eagle Creek after he was murdered by robbers in the dead of winter. His body didn't surface until Eagle pushed out of its banks, flooding, in the spring.

Mostly, though, Eagle Creek was a benevolent presence in our lives. Even in the driest months, it provided enough water for our cattle and to irrigate the crops. Over time, it had made our bottomland rich and fertile. We swam in the creek too, and fished and paddled.

And so when I read on the Owen County Government's website that my Eagle is the longest creek in the world, I believed them. It seems as though it should be. It was, after all, only one mile short of claiming its rightful place among the earth's rivers.

Forget Anastasia and the Lost Dauphin of France—Eagle Creek's royalty finally had been acknowledged. Giddy, I set out to verify this local claim to worldwide fame. My enthusiasm was soon deflated. I learned that Eagle Creek does ramble for 87 miles through five Kentucky counties before it flows into the Kentucky River at Worthville. This is not far before the Kentucky, in turn, flows into the great Ohio, and the confluence of Big Eagle and the Kentucky River is impressive. With a little research, however, I quickly identified other creeks in America—much less the world—that are longer than 87 miles. Among those are Ohio's Raccoon Creek that measures 109, and Crab Creek in Washington State that stretches to a 175 miles. I couldn't even document that my Eagle is the longest creek in Kentucky.

Then, insult added to injury, I learned that five other Kentucky streams are named Eagle Creek, too. I felt like crying.

Perhaps, though, the old claim that it had missed being a river by only a mile was true. Alas, I could find no rule any-

8

where that requires a river to be a certain length. Indeed, I identified a good many that are said to be shorter than 87 miles. I concluded that joining the fraternity of rivers may have more to do with the whims of words than with length.

Over a lifetime, my horizon expanded beyond the row of sycamores on the creek's bank. Change, some of it good, some of it not, came to the Eagle Creek valleys, too, and to the people who live there.

Still, when they say Eagle Creek is the longest creek in the world, I believe them. With a little more help from God—or a little more respect from the likes of Daniel Boone or Simon Kenton—it could have been a river you know.

"This is the most beautiful place on earth. There are many such places. Every man, every woman, carries in heart and mind the image of the ideal place, the right place, the one true home, known or unknown, actual or visionary."

—Edward Abbey in *Desert Solitaire*

The Past Is Never Dead

"The past is never dead. It's not even past." William Faulkner wrote that. I'm not sure I know what the line means. Faulkner's mind was complex and his words nuanced and layered. But he was born in Mississippi in 1897 where the Civil War could break loose again at the turn of a prepositional phrase over supper most any night of the week. And I was born in Owen County, Kentucky, where we identify the names of fields on our farm by the names of men a century dead.

So I think I may know what Faulkner was talking about. At least, I remembered his words last Memorial Day weekend when my father's family gathered at the Poplar Grove Cemetery, as it has done for over one hundred years, to decorate the grave of our Uncle Laurel who died in 1906 at the age of two.

Later, our grandparents, Frank and Rushia Green, were buried beside their firstborn child, and we come now to honor them, but it is Laurel's story that began the ritual. In ways I cannot quite explain, I believe his brief life strengthened and shaped who the Greens became as a family.

Mawmaw and Pawpaw Green were blessed with long and productive lives. Pawpaw lived well into his 90s and mowed his own lawn with a push mower through the last summer of his life. Mawmaw died fifteen years before he did, but still—though she did not marry until her mid-twenties—she lived to see seven of her eight children reach middle age, lived to see grandchildren grown and married, and cradled great-grandchildren in her arms.

Laurel's life, however, ended soon after it began. In 1906, when he was two years old, he took ill with dysentery, and within a few days he died of dehydration. For the rest of her life, my grandmother blamed herself for his death. He had wandered from her in the yard and eaten nameless wild berries, and she was sure the fruit—and her inattention—had caused the diarrhea. The doctor said probably not, and dismissed her guilt. Even so, I was a more careful mother because of Mawmaw's often-repeated story.

"But Laurel is my only child," I hear Mawmaw crying.

"You will have more," the doctor said, as he placed nickels on the boy's eyelids, closing them forever.

I do not know if he spoke in platitudes, or if he spoke with the certainty of a country doctor who had stood by generations of such deathbeds and had glimpsed the future many times over. But he was right. They had seven more children, including five more sons. Each was healthy and smart, and lived a good, long life. Today, Mawmaw and Pawpaw Green have over a hundred living descendants, and it's likely their biological seed will endure until the end of time.

Yet every May for over a century, our family has placed flowers on Laurel's grave, honoring, grieving, the life this one child did not get to live. In the beginning, of course, it was our grandparents who came. They pulled brambles and weeds away from his grave, and helped others in the farm community clean the cemetery on top of the ridge, pulling it back from the hayfield it yearned to be.

Later, Laurel's brothers helped with this spring work. My cousin Bob, the oldest of the grandchildren, recalls coming as a child with his uncles and with Pawpaw to tend the grave. Now, hired grounds keepers with modern mowing equipment do the work for us, and we no longer need to come with a scythe. Instead, we come only with flowers.

My cousin Kaye places a single red rose on Laurel's grave because that is what her daddy, my Uncle Woodrow, always did. Each of us places something, nothing much, something simple, an iris maybe, but something. This year, we were all mindful that Uncle Nevel, my grandparents' second child, was absent. He made this pilgrimage with us a year ago. He was 101 and a half last May, sound of mind and making jokes, but his body was frail and we would lose him in August.

There are historical plaques for houses that stand stout and firm for a century or more, but I've never heard of an award for a family that decorates a child's grave continuously for over a hundred years. We're probably not the only family in Kentucky, though, that holds such a record. I admit, it's not too hard for us to gather because we've not scattered far geographically, and we enjoy the talk and food that always follows.

Still, I'm not entirely sure why we do it. We come, I know, because we loved our grandparents, and maybe because we remember finding the nickels that closed Laurel's eyes hidden in a little sack in Mawmaw's drawer when we were children. We come because we are parents and grandparents ourselves, because we understand loss, and are thankful it was Mawmaw's and not our own. We come because we love each other, to renew our vows in a silent ceremony by a tombstone.

And maybe, it has something to do with our hope that we, too, can build families that endure, that will stand stout and firm and together for a century or more.

The Summer I Was Ten

L ast July, Hattie Hunter's long life ended. I hold many memories close that celebrate her journey across this earth—such a funny, strong, hard-working country woman. But when I stood at her bed a day before she slipped into her final coma, she insisted on talking about me, not herself, and a long ago July afternoon when her heart had wept for mine. It was her final gift of love, to remember with me what no one else now living can.

The summer I was ten, Death showed up uninvited at our front door and refused to leave. It wasn't that I had not been introduced to him before. Growing up on a farm, I learned what buzzards circling in the sky meant almost before I could talk. Something was always dying, a groundhog or wild rabbit, or a ewe leaving an orphaned lamb for me to raise as a pet on a bottle. And per custom of the time and place, I tagged along with my parents wherever they went, attending more funerals in my first decade than some people do in a lifetime.

By ten, a precocious only child who read too much, I'd learned the language Death spoke, about those at peace in a better place, beyond the sunset or gathered by the river, because it was God's will, may it ever be done, amen, amen. My beloved Gran Hudson, whose home had been my own since the day of my birth, had died the year before, the spring I turned nine. He'd been ill with a devastating disease for a year or longer before his death, however, and even as I grieved for him, I understood that he was out of pain. Before that, the year I turned eight, Mother had been sent to bed for months before the stillborn birth of my sister. Mother was allowed to hold Baby Becky in the hospital, and she said she looked exactly like me when I was born. Words hadn't come easy to explain Becky's death, but Mother had been so ill, perhaps it was "just as well" she said because "Becky might have been sick too" or "not right."

Georgia's Paternal Grandparents: Mawmaw Green holding a great-grandchild; standing, l-r, her son Nevel/Bo, who would live to be 101, daughter-in-law Alberta, and Pawpaw Green who lived to be almost 94. Circa 1953.

All of this was behind us, however, as we began 1955. The year arrived with wonderful news. Mother would be having a baby in early September. This time, Mother did not get sick, and everything was good and right with the baby as it grew inside her. Mother and Daddy were happy, and so was I.

In a coincidence that seemed to me ordained by God, Mable Dean, my age and my nearest playmate, was also getting a new baby at her house that summer. Although she had two older siblings, she was as excited about losing her spot as the baby of the family as I was about shedding my only-ness. Though we were a tad old to be playing dolls, she and I took in practicing to be big sisters with a passion. On pretty afternoons straight out of a storybook, we played house under ancient trees. The elms' gnarly roots pushed out of the ground, and shaped pretend rooms where we sat caring for our dollies until supper called us home.

I'm not sure when my Mawmaw Green began slipping off to play with make-believe babies, too. It seemed to happen over-night, but perhaps dementia had been creeping up on her for a long time, and I'd been unaware of change. Suddenly, though, she didn't recognize me, or any of us. Instead, she spent all her days and nights in her old rocking chair, cradling imaginary babies in her arms, shushing them, and singing lullabies.

"It's all she's ever done," Mother reminded Daddy and his six siblings.

Playing with dolls didn't feel the same to me anymore.

Mable Dean lost interest in our fantasy world, too, when her real baby brother arrived, and so I turned my attention to my new record player and to rock 'n roll. Over the long, hot weeks my grandmother spent slowly moving toward death, softly singing her invisible children to sleep, my cousins and I rocked around the clock with Bill Haley. We jumped and twisted in my grand-parents' seldom used and shut-off front parlor, until we col-lapsed, exhausted, on their horsehair Murphy fold-down bed.

Finally, there came a night when the grown-ups sent us up the lane to eat and sleep with those who'd asked, "What can we do to help?" There, in the final hours of my grandmother's life, we ran in the dark, chasing lightning bugs and the neighbors' children, and I was as happy as I've ever been. Mother came, then, in the morning, and took me to town to buy new patent leather maryjanes. "Shoes for the funeral," she said.

At the end of July, a few weeks after my grandmother's death, Mother called out to me from her bedroom. "Go get help," she said. The look of fear and pain on her face brooked no questions. We didn't have a telephone in those days, almost no one did, and Daddy was off who knew where measuring tobacco with the part-time government job he'd taken with the ASC to earn extra money for Mother's hospital stay ahead.

I ran as fast as Black Beauty, my feet pounding the gravel country road, my breath coming in gasps, to first one house and then another, until at last I found Hattie Hunter at home, a half mile or more down the lane, and poured out my story, come, help, come, please.

Hattie gathered me and another nearby neighbor into her car, and soon I was home again. I turned it over, then, to them to help Mother. I did not understand how difficult their challenge was.

The old covered bridge over Eagle Creek at Natlee had been destroyed by fire the year before, and the new concrete bridge was not yet completed. To get help, Hattie went to the edge of the creek and hollered and yelled until someone at the Natlee Store—the location of the closest telephone—could be roused. The storekeeper called the Funeral Home in Corinth, which doubled as the ambulance service, but the ambulance, because the bridge was out, had to detour by way of Frogtown, miles out of the way, to reach Mother.

In time—an hour, two—Mother was lifted into the ambulance and then whisked over a labyrinth of bumpy back roads to a Lexington hospital. My little brother was already dead, of course. He would never take a breath. But I didn't know that. I thought I had saved him and Mother too by my heroic dash for help.

I went home with Hattie to wait for the big news. Daddy didn't come until the next afternoon. He asked me to sit with him in the wide double swing on Hattie's porch. At first, I couldn't believe what he was telling me. I had a brother, but he died? Mother was awful sick, but she'd be okay? And then I said, well maybe next year Mother will have another baby, but Daddy said no. No, not ever again.

That's when I began to cry. I tried not to for Daddy's sake, but I couldn't help myself. I cried and cried and cried for the life my brother would never live. I cried for me because I would never be a sister. I cried for Mawmaw Green and Gran Hudson and for my baby sister, Becky. I cried because I was ten years old and I was flat out of words.

Soon Daddy left to return to Mother, and Hattie held me in her arms and never let go of me again. She held me in her heart for the rest of her life as though I were one of hers. In time, I would lose others close to me, even an unborn baby of my own, then Daddy, then Mother, but Hattie remained with me.

Then last July, the inevitable call came from her son. Her kidneys, worn out from years of struggle with diabetes, had failed that morning, and her ailing heart would not support dialysis. I hung up the phone and without changing clothes or combing my hair drove straight to the hospital as quickly as she had come to me a lifetime earlier when I had called out for help. Yet, I had no help to offer other than my presence. What would I even say?

I need not have worried. From the minute I stepped into her room, Hattie began to talk, excited to see me, laughing even. It was as though the awareness of her imminent death had released her to live in that moment. She reminisced about my parents, and the good times they'd had together. She repeated a poignant story about my father that she'd shared with me many times before, concluding as she always did with the statement, "Dexter was an awful good man."

But most of all, she was eager to re-visit that intersection of life and death and love where we had stood together a lifetime earlier, a place that cannot be described to others who have not been there with you, somewhere you have to experience to understand. She wanted to talk about that long ago July day when I'd sat in her front porch swing, and her heart had broken for me.

And then she said, "I love you, Georgia."

"I love you, too, Hattie."

She held my hand tight.

I love you.

I love you too.

Daddy

Bad fathers, from King Lear to Huckleberry Finn's Pap, get more attention in literature, it seems to me, than good ones. The Bible warns us, though, that the sins of the fathers are visited on the children even unto the third and fourth generation, stalking families, cursing them, haunting memory. Perhaps twisted men, like the narcissistic Lear or the drunken Pap, leave behind a legacy so toxic it can only be excised with the power of words, with the purity of poetry.

Still, it troubles me that the influence of good fathers is not celebrated more in letters. From a lifetime of reading, I finally pulled up Atticus Finch as an example of a great literary dad, a sort of Anti-Pap-Finn. Surely there are others in the pages of books, but Atticus is who came to my mind, maybe because he reminds me of my own father.

Daddy was a Kentucky tobacco farmer, not an eloquent lawyer like Atticus, and he didn't look or sound anything like the magnificent Gregory Peck who won an Oscar for that role in the movie version of *To Kill A Mockingbird*. But Atticus Finch was a believable character to me because I was raised by Dexter Green.

In a curious way, I think I began writing because of my father, my Atticus, so that I could hear his voice in my head again after he died. Daddy cut through pretense wherever he ran across it, and homed in on what was genuine. He could spot the absurd in any situation, and get everybody laughing about it, thinking about it. And so I believe I write to hear him tell a story again. Maybe I even hope—though he's been gone over twenty

19

years—that he'll whisper, yes, Georgia, you're getting there, you're learning, you've just about got it right this time.

Georgia's Wedding: Georgia and her father; her Green cousins, twins Bonnie and Connie, assisted by her cousin Georgia Vincent.

But I've had trouble writing about Daddy straight on. Like all originals, he's slippery on paper, defying easy images. He was a tallish man, even as I'm a tallish woman, and yet I think he had to stretch to reach six feet. Perhaps it was his insistence on good posture for both himself and me that made him seem taller than he was. When I was growing up, he would encourage me to practice walking with a book balanced on my head. "Tall girls can't slump," he'd say, and so I didn't.

Although everyone tells me I'm the spitting image of Mother, I always thought I looked more like him. His hair, when he had some, was blonde, and in the set of his blue eyes and the narrowness of his mouth, I see my own. And if I have a memory for story or detail, it is a pale reflection of his.

Despite his flair for storytelling, he was, when I think about it, a quiet man, reserved. Yet men who were young when my father died, tell me even now that they quote Dexter "all the time." When I press them for examples, they shrug, and glance away as though embarrassed at their seriousness, and say, "Oh, you know, things about living life." And so I have a glimpse of my father as a philosopher in the tobacco fields influencing the men who worked alongside him.

He was a man who more often sought the sidelines than the spotlight, but then I remember his boisterous laugh. A whooping affair that could be heard a block away, it punctuated all his stories, and it was wonderful, I realize now, the kind of laugh that got everyone else laughing too. But it embarrassed me when I was a kid. You never wanted to see a funny movie with Daddy—not if you didn't want everybody in the theater to turn their heads and stare at you.

With the exception of the few years he spent at Georgetown College and in the Army Air Corps, Daddy farmed all his life. He respected the land, and was an environmentalist before the word came into vogue, leaving his place on earth better than he found it. He must have served on the Owen County Soil Conservation Board for forty years. Yet I never thought he enjoyed the business of farming. He didn't have the passion for it that my mother had.

I'm not sure what livelihood Daddy would have preferred over farming. If there were a job that would have paid him for reading—remember Li'l Abner who napped all day testing mattresses?—he might have liked that. He would come in from the fields every night, settle in his easy chair, and read a book. That is my most enduring memory of him. And so I grew up assuming that reading was an everyday ritual, like eating.

Daddy was a considerate man, too, who never wanted to put anybody out so I know he would have been mortified at the commotion his death caused. His tractor overturned on a steep hill below the barn on a rainy January day, and it took hours for his body to be recovered. Somewhere, I'm sure his spirit is still apologizing to his friends and neighbors for the trouble he caused them.

More than considerate, he was also tender-hearted. Many stories come to my mind, but one that haunts me is the time his BushHog ran over a newborn calf hidden in the undergrowth. Daddy took it so hard, we nearly had to bury him that morning. The men who were working with him repeated that story to me one after another at his funeral, shaking their heads as they remembered his anguish.

As for me, he never refused to do anything I asked him to do. Forty-five years ago, Ernie and I were married in the small Methodist Church near our farm. It was a simple wedding open to everyone, but I'd been off to college by then and was starting to have highfaluting notions. I wanted a fine bakery cake brought in from Frankfort for the reception. And so Daddy set off in his pick-up truck to carry home a cake wide enough and tall enough to feed two or three hundred folks. How he managed to get it there intact over forty miles of the crookedest roads in Kentucky, I'll never know. But he did it without a complaint—even though he personally thought people should simply "go to the court-house and not worry everybody to death" when they wanted to get married.

Daddy wasn't perfect of course. He could lose his temper—never at people—but at things when they broke. He was too often quiet when he should have spoken, giving in to others on things that didn't matter in his opinion in order to avoid conflict. And sometimes he was outspoken in his opinion when he should have remained silent, a wise man talking to fools who couldn't hear. Yet, he was as fine a father as I could have ordered up.

And surely, if a father's sins can reverberate for generations, surely, surely, a father's goodness echoes through time.

Georgia's Maternal Grandfather: George/Gran Hudson, left; Great-uncle Murphy Hudson and Great-aunt Bessie Hudson; Georgia and her cousin James Hudson. Circa 1953

Jesse Stuart, the Bookmobile and Me

Even though I loved to read, I hadn't heard of the Appalachian writer, Jesse Stuart, until Ralph Edwards surprised him on the television show, "This Is Your Life." That was in 1958, and I'd lived all of my thirteen years on earth in Kentucky. I was amazed that I didn't know about Jesse Stuart, and I was dazzled that a fellow Kentuckian was celebrated on national television. I had no clue that night, however, that I would bump into Stuart's long shadow for years to come. Indeed, as I sat on the living room floor staring at our small black and white television set, Jesse had already changed my life.

Even so, it took another ten years before I got around to reading one of his books. By the 1960s, when I was in high school and college, both Stuart's popular appeal and his literary reputation were waning, and he was never mentioned by any of my instructors. Straight out of college, however, I was offered a job teaching English and speech at a high school down the road from Stuart's W Hollow. I moved from another part of the state and took up residence in Jesse Stuart country.

When I came across one of Stuart's stories anthologized in our Harcourt & Brace textbook, I scared my sleepy students with my excitement. How could I explain to them that the inclusion of our neighbor in such a book had knocked the breath out of this wanna-be writer? If Jesse could make it, writing about our place, could I?

That same year, I stood in line at Parson's Department Store in downtown Ashland to have Jesse Stuart autograph a copy of his masterpiece, *The Thread That Runs So True*. It chronicles his

24

first year of teaching, but I was too intimidated to tell him that I was a beginning teacher, myself. I was so nervous, I could barely stammer out that it was a Father's Day present for my dad. I certainly didn't tell him that Daddy, like him, was a farmer who loved to read, a poet of the soil as Stuart had described his own father. It was the only gift I ever gave Daddy that made his eyes light up. I'll never forget his fondling the book, and saying in a quiet, near awe-struck voice, "I've never owned a book signed by the author before."

I wish I'd had sense enough to write Jesse and tell him how much Daddy loved that present. From what I know now about his willingness to encourage young writers and teachers, I feel sure he would have written back, and a friendship with my famous neighbor could have been established. But I was too timid to do that. He was old and famous. I was young and insecure. Jesse slipped back into the shadows of my life where I glimpsed him from time to time eating in the dining room at the Jesse Stuart Lodge at Greenbo State Park or leaving a commercial establishment as I was entering.

Fifteen years later, I served as a trustee on the Greenup County Library Board, an organization first chaired by Jesse Stuart. Our pride at having a big name writer in our library lineage was evident in the long shelf of his autographed first editions in the regional book collection. Framed drawings and art prints of his home hung on the walls of all our branch buildings, and Stuart's name was often invoked as we tried to stay true to the library's mission.

However, it was not until a year or so ago, in correspondence with longtime Greenup County librarian, Dorothy Griffith, that I learned Stuart had literally talked Kentucky's modern bookmobile system into existence. Like an old-time camp meeting evangelist, he had stood in a gilded Louisville ballroom, and pleaded for the salvation of Kentucky's poor children who were "hungry for books." His fiery words hit their target, the hearts of Kentucky's elite gathered to organize Friends of Kentucky Libraries. In a single afternoon, a polite, institutional gathering was transformed into a passionate group. Within less than two years, Jesse would see a mile long caravan of rolling libraries on the move to serve his beloved school children.

Once again, I felt as though I'd had the breath knocked out of me. If Jesse's rhetoric fueled the fleet of bookmobiles that took to the highways of rural Kentucky in the fall of 1954, then he had, indeed, changed the course of my life.

One of the first of those funny looking mint green bread trucks stuffed with books had sputtered to a stop in the graveled parking lot of three-room New Columbus Grade School. Afterwards, I was never the same. Maybe I would have gotten to college anyway. Maybe I would have majored in English if I had. But I cannot imagine that I would be the same person without the hundreds—maybe thousands—of books I plucked from the bookmobile's shelves during my growing up years. How had Jesse Stuart known how hungry I was for books? There simply weren't any in my elementary school except for the few textbooks the county school board provided, and the nearest library was twenty miles away over curvy roads.

Even now, I can remember the tingling sensation in my stomach whenever I was chosen to assist the teacher select the school's bi-weekly "book drop" from the bookmobile's shelves. It was a great honor to be asked to help the teacher choose the fifty or so books that my classmates and I would have available to read until the library-on-wheels returned in two weeks. I assumed my responsibility with seriousness.

Books still vaguely smell like the bookmobile to me, with its exhaust fumes permeating the tight bookshelves that stretched from floorboard to roof. I can see the blue backed biographies about the childhoods of famous Americans—Clara Barton, George Washington, Eli Whitney, Booker T. Washington, Andrew Jackson—and I remember how I yearned to make a difference, too, when I grew up. Memory caresses the classic children's novels like *Heidi* and *Swiss Family Robinson* plucked from a low shelf. *Heidi* was the first book that made me cry. Like her, I'd been homesick, too, when my mother was gravely ill and I was left with relatives for weeks. And the Robinsons—I marveled at their resourcefulness. They became a model for surviving and coping with adversity. I reach once more for the books about dinosaurs—oh, there were more mysteries on the earth than I had suspected.

The world had navigated curvy, old Highway 330, then bumped down graveled KY 607 to stop and pick me up for the ride. Never mind that there were only about 70 students in all eight grades of New Columbus Grade School, or that we had no hot lunch cafeteria, no central heat, no indoor toilet, or for that matter no toilet paper in the outhouse. With books, we could get as fine an education as we were willing to reach for. With books, we could go anywhere.

"Jesse Stuart was thrilled about the bookmobile program," Mrs. Griffith wrote in her e-mail, "and felt he was instrumental in its inception." In 1960, Mrs. Griffith was personally recruited by Jesse Stuart to oversee Greenup County's six-year-old bookmobile service. She went on to cite a 1979 Bookmobile Newsletter published by the Kentucky Department of Library and Archives. The Newsletter credits Stuart's 1952 speech at the organizational meeting of Friends of Kentucky Libraries in Louisville as the inspiration for the modern Kentucky bookmobile movement.

Surprised by this information, I quickly Googled the word "bookmobile" and located a 2004 article in *The Courier-Journal* written by James Nelson, Kentucky State Librarian. While the bookmobile concept traces its roots to several early efforts such as "The Traveling Book Project" initiated by Mrs. C. P. Barnes in 1887, Berea College's 1917 "Bookwagon" and the WPA Packhorse Library Project in 1934, Nelson gives Jesse Stuart much of the credit for Kentucky's modern bookmobile system.

"There is no question," Nelson writes, "that the real genesis of the state's famous fleet of bookmobiles occurred at the organizational meeting of the Friends of Kentucky Libraries in 1952. It was at this meeting that Kentucky author Jessie Stuart made an inspirational speech about the reading needs of rural families, and his comments got the right people motivated in the way that movements need to succeed."

Louisville businessman, Harry Schacter, president of the Kaufman-Straus Department stores, was sitting in the audience that September day when Jesse Stuart stepped to the platform to speak to a joint session of the Kentucky Library Association and the newly formed volunteer Friends group. Schacter was not elected to an office in the new Friends organization, and I've been unable to find a public record of his direct involvement with libraries prior to this event. I suspect he was invited to the downtown luncheon meeting because of his position within the Louisville business community. He had also been involved earlier with the by then defunct Committee For Kentucky, a non-partisan political organization in the years just after World War II.

Stuart was at his peak in the fall of 1952, and it seems significant that KLA chose him as their headline speaker to attract community leaders such as Schacter to the Friends organizational session. His masterpiece, *The Thread That Runs So True*, had been published in 1949 to both critical and popular acclaim, and Stuart, an outstanding public speaker, was in great demand on the dais of education-related groups throughout the country. However, the contrast between Stuart's rural, eastern Kentucky and Louisville's neo-European, ornate Seelbach hotel could not have been starker. More significantly, the access to books and education available to the children who populated Stuart's short stories and novels was vastly different than that enjoyed by the privileged Kentuckians gathered in the Seelbach's gilded ballroom.

Unfortunately, the text of Stuart's speech that day has not survived. Perhaps he didn't have a manuscript since he was a skillful extemporaneous speaker. But we know that he told his audience that eighty percent of rural Kentuckians did not have access to library service—a situation shared by sixty percent of all Kentuckians. We know that he told them only North Dakota did a worse job than Kentucky when it came to getting books distributed to its citizens. We know that he spoke of the children's "hunger for books" because that phrase was repeated in newspaper accounts of the speech. We know that Stuart, the teacher, would have reminded his audience of Kentucky's shameful illiteracy rate. We know—because this was Jesse Stuart—that he talked for a long time, that he poured his heart and soul into his words, that he talked as if the future of the state depended on what he said that day. We know that when he finished speaking, Harry Schacter was an inspired man. Jesse Stuart had set him on fire.

Schacter had both the means and the connections to move mountains. In this case, he set about moving mountains of books to the mountains of Kentucky—and to all other rural areas of the state. He quickly recruited Mary Bingham, wife of Barry Bingham the powerful editor of *The Courier-Journal*, to spearhead the bookmobile effort. In short order, the likes of Vice-President Albin Barkley, Governor Lawrence Wetherby, former Governor Happy Chandler, Senators John Sherman Cooper and Earle Clements, most of the state's newspaper editors, and literary notables such as Robert Penn Warren and A. B. Guthrie jumped on board the bookmobile bandwagon.

Within less than two years, over $300,000 dollars were raised to purchase bookmobiles, and hundreds of thousands of books had been donated. Eighty-four bookmobiles—reportedly they stretched along the route for a solid mile—were presented to the Library Extension Service at the State Fair in the fall of 1954. By the end of 1955, 102 were in service. According to State Librarian James Nelson, Kentucky has been the national leader in bookmobile service ever since.

An achievement of this magnitude cannot be attributed solely to one person, even a larger than life personality like Jesse Stuart. Hundreds of concerned individuals took his words and ran with them. Eventually, thousands of involved people made the bookmobile fleet a reality for children such as me. However, public speaking and literature were the dual enthusiasms of my youth—I concentrated my studies in college on both and later taught both—and so I love the symbolism of Stuart's speech bringing books into my life.

There is a granite monument dedicated to Jesse Stuart in the courthouse square in Greenup. I have to think that the vibrant fleet of Kentucky bookmobiles is a more fitting memorial. The mile long line of book trucks that pulled onto Kentucky's roads in 1954 is a powerful image of education moving forward. It is right and fitting that Jesse Stuart, the consummate teacher and master of both spoken and written language, was at the wheel.

"Monuments fall, nations perish. Civilizations grow old and die out. And after an era of darkness new races build others. But in the world of books are volumes that have seen this happen again and again, and yet live on still young, still as fresh as the day they were written, still telling men's hearts of the hearts of men centuries dead." —Jesse Stuart

The 1940 Election

I read about two brothers over in the western part of the state who got into an argument over the presidential election and ended up shooting each other. No one in my family ever shot each other in a political argument as far as I know, unless the Civil War counts. Then it was brother against brother in lots of Kentucky homes. But on Daddy's side, I do descend from a mixed political marriage, and election discord is part of my heritage. My grandparents' political differences probably did have their beginnings in the Civil War. Pawpaw's father, John William Green, fought in uniform for the Confederacy, but many of Mawmaw's relatives stood firm by the Union.

However he may have arrived at his political persuasion, Pawpaw Green would vote for a yeller dog if it ran as a Democrat, and his esteem for FDR approached idolatry. He even slept with a photograph of Franklin Roosevelt nailed above the bed he shared with Mawmaw. He'd clipped the picture from a newspaper and framed it, and it decorated their bedroom wall for as long as anyone now living can remember. When Pawpaw died in 1970 at the age of ninety-three, FDR was still with him, hanging over the cherry double bed. How Mawmaw Green may have felt about sleeping under FDR's gaze for decades has been lost to history.

What we do know is this. When the United States saw fit to give Mawmaw the constitutional right to vote in 1920, she registered as a Republican. By then she was forty-one years old. Forty-one years old—that takes my breath away, and for her sake, this granddaughter has never passed up an opportunity to vote.

Perhaps she went Republican to distinguish her thinking from her husband's, to celebrate the independent spirit of women's suffrage. She was an intelligent woman, a school-teacher in her youth, and her circumstances as a farmer's wife had given her little chance to do anything other than rock babies, cook, and survive.

Whatever may have influenced their divergent political affiliations, my grandparents' household was always tense at election time, especially every four years when the country chose a president. Matters didn't reach a crisis, however, until 1940 when FDR sought an unprecedented third term, and the GOP yielded to its suicide wish and nominated the dark horse Wendell Willkie.

Willkie was the worst sort of Republican in Pawpaw's opinion. Willkie was a turncoat, a man who'd been a Democrat until 1939, who'd given money to FDR's previous campaigns! Pawpaw placed him in the same category as Benedict Arnold.

Moreover, Willkie—president of America's largest electric holding company—had the audacity to question the legality of TVA. TVA had brought rural electrification into Pawpaw's Kentucky home. "When nobody else would," Pawpaw always added in a loud voice punctuated by his fist pounding the table. Willkie had never held political office either, and Pawpaw was aghast that anyone would consider voting for such an inexperienced and misguided man.

Mawmaw, on the other hand, was uneasy about electing Roosevelt for a third term. Willkie's slogan resonated with her: if one man is indispensable, then none of us is free. And maybe he did have a point about the government funded TVA unfairly competing with private utilities. It didn't hurt that Willkie was handsome and young, only forty-eight, and from nearby Indiana, too.

And finally, listening on her radio late into the night, her imagination had been captured by Willkie's out of nowhere selection on the sixth ballot at the GOP convention. His nomination is still considered one of the most dramatic stories in American political history. Maybe he'd been touched by Destiny's hand, Mawmaw said.

So it went throughout the fall and into the weeks leading up to the November election. But there came a night when Pawpaw could not take this silly babble about Destiny any longer. Pushed to the brink of reason by his wife's stubborn support of wishy-washy Willkie, Pawpaw shouted, "I cannot sleep with that Republican!" And he stomped out of the house and moved into the tobacco-stripping room, a dusty shack attached to the barn.

My cousin Bob recalls that Pawpaw slept in the stripping room for at least three nights. What Bob does not remember is whether Mawmaw removed FDR's picture from her bedroom wall during Pawpaw's absence.

In time, Pawpaw returned to the house. Sleeping with a Republican was apparently less uncomfortable than lying with dried tobacco and a quilt on the stripping room's hard, dirty floor. FDR was re-elected, and my grandparents continued to live together until death did them part after fifty-two years and a houseful of descendants.

Despite having heard this family story repeated many times, I didn't include "same political party affiliation" on my criteria list when I went looking for a helpmate. As it turns out, my husband and I have rarely agreed on a candidate in forty-five years of marriage, and presidential elections have often been as tense for us as they were for Mawmaw and Pawpaw Green. At the end of the day, however, we remember that the stripping room floor is not a comfortable place to sleep.

A Tobacco Kind of Christmas

For a hundred years, maybe two hundred, my Owen County family relied on growing tobacco for their economic health. Of course, they did not know how unhealthy smoking was for their bodies, but even understanding that as I do now, I am stunned that within a handful of years, six-bent barns have come to stand empty. Fertile fields lie fallow. And the mammoth tobacco auction warehouses that once dominated towns like Carrollton, Cynthiana, and Lexington have become, like dinosaurs, extinct overnight.

My childhood memories of Christmastime intertwine with the tobacco market like conjoined twins, making it difficult for me to separate one from the other. The "Sears Wish Catalog" would arrive the week after Thanksgiving, and I would sit, then, in a corner of the stripping room with its colored pictures spread on my lap while my parents worked twelve-hour days to make my wishes come true. Preparing the tobacco for market was next to the final step in an economic process that had begun in the early spring.

The final step, of course, was selling the tobacco. My family usually opted to take our crop to Lexington, which claimed to be the largest burley tobacco market in the world. I have no reason to think the Chamber of Commerce was exaggerating. All over town, gigantic auction warehouses came right up to the edge of busy thoroughfares like South Broadway and Fourth Street, a visual statement of the enormous economic impact tobacco held for Lexington businessmen as well as the region's farmers.

Now, the old warehouses have been torn down or gentrified into loft apartments. Tobacco has become a villain, and few mourn the demise of the auction and government price support system that sustained it. The tobacco warehouses and auctions linger only in footnotes—like flatboats on the Kentucky River— and in the memories of farm kids like me.

In the Tobacco Patch: Georgia's father,
Dexter Green, right.

The burley tobacco market (not to be confused with North Carolina's flue-cured market) opened in early December on a date calculated to be the coldest of the year. The cavernous buildings were walled with cheap sheets of tin that did little more than infuriate the wind, and a damp chill oozed up through the concrete floors until feet went numb and the roots of the hair on the head froze stiff.

Despite the frigid temperatures, excitement electrified us when we heard the auctioneer's rapid-fire chant echo off the high rafters. He moved up and down the mile-long aisles stacked with dry, brown tobacco, pausing only a few moments at each person's crop. We held our breath when he finally came to our baskets—which were not exactly baskets but woven pallets that cupped shoulder-high hills of crisp tobacco "hands," small bundles of leaves neatly tied together. A year's work hung in the balance of a single minute. Our hearts beat so loud we couldn't be sure of the agreed on price as the auctioneer, speaking in his rapid, near-foreign language moved on to sell another family's sweat and tears to the highest bidder.

Only then could we rush forward to see the sale price the buyer had written on the tag.

Only then could we leave the rank smelling place.

The odor of the dried tobacco leaves was so intense in those warehouses that it cannot be described in olfactory terms. It was something more than smell, a strident presence that seemed to take on three-dimensional shape like a beam holding up the roof. Or it could have been a living thing, an aggressive virus that invaded our nostrils, settling deep into our lungs. We ran from it as we left the warehouse, and drank in the crisp outdoors to purge ourselves, as thirsty for clean cold air as we had been for ice water in the August fields.

Euphoria welled within us as we drove downtown where the fine stores lined up along Main Street. We would spend freely for one time during the year, on Christmas gifts and small luxuries, a new electric Mixmaster for my mother, or maybe a transistor radio for me. We would eat at Walgreen's Drugstore— the "all you can eat" fried fish in a basket was always my choice—or at Purcell's Department Store's more genteel cafeteria with its fancy fruit salads and fluffy desserts.

Years later I would learn that the Woolworth's I thought was so wonderful really was wonderful, a magnificent example of art deco architecture. Ditto for the Kentucky and Ben Ali movie theaters. I would learn that the Phoenix Hotel with its canopy that stretched from door to street, its uniformed doormen, and its thick-carpeted lobby was a pretty good version of a first class hotel anywhere. Lowenthal's fur-filled windows and Embry's vestibule heavy with the scent of an expensive perfume were as hoity-toity as shops I'd later see in much larger cities in other parts of the world.

But the burley warehouses that dominated the city's streetscape were unique to Kentucky, even as the tobacco fields that defined the countryside were unique. Drafty temples of commerce, the warehouses anchored an economic system that was nigh-on a religion, sustaining a tribe of people and the land they loved.

Now Lexington's old warehouses are gone, and the fields on our Owen County farm have not grown tobacco for close to a decade. Little girls don't sit and dream with the Sears Wish Book on their lap watching their parents prepare the crop for the December market. A tobacco kind of Christmas lingers only in the memories of people like me.

The Night the Old House
Burned Down

On a May midnight when I was four, the farmhouse my parents and I shared with my Grandfather, George "Gran" Hudson, exploded. We escaped with only our nightclothes and our lives. Like a curtain rising at the beginning of a play about the rest of my life, my clear memory begins the night the old house burned down.

Although the fire would divide the timeline of my family's history, our experience was not remarkable. Heating stoves with faulty flues and jackleg wiring retrofitted to electrify our old houses lay in wait in the rural countryside like arsonists on the loose. With little water and no equipment, we were helpless when the random fires struck. Nearly every year, at least one family in the area watched its home burn to rubble.

Over six decades later, emotion still swamps me when my mind re-visits the spring night our house melted into ashes. I find it easier to write about the fire from the distance of fiction, in a voice that is not quite mine. Here, in an excerpt from an autobiographical novel in progress, I'm heard in the voice of the child, Shirley. My parents and grandfather are named, but other characters, such as Fannie, Oriole and C. C. Lee are imaginary, composites of the many who stood beside us that awful night.

Before the house burned, there had been a ton of pictures everybody said. But now there were none. Everybody talked about their lives before the fire a lot, so that time seemed real to Shirley, but there weren't any photographs of it. No baby pictures of her. No pictures of the old house. Nothing. Shirley thought it was like earth before the flood in the bible—wiped out except in stories. After Noah came out of the ark with all the animals, two by two, life went on, but nothing was ever the same in the world again. After the flood. After the fire.

Shirley's memories of the time before the house burned were like shadows, here, then there. But after the house burned, Shirley remembered everything as plainly as last week's episode of The Lone Ranger on television.

The night of the fire, Shirley had been four years, three weeks, and two days old. She was sleeping—they were all sleeping—when they heard a big boom and then Daddy lifted her from her narrow bed and carried her through the dark of the house into the dark of the night. He sat her down by the front yard gate.

"Don't move, Shirley. Stay put. You understand? Stay put!"

And then he ran back into the house yelling for Gran Hudson.

Shirley was too scared to cry. This wasn't right. She was standing outside near the road in the middle of the night in her nightgown. She didn't even have any shoes on. Then she saw Mama running from somewhere into the house.

"The keys to the car," Mama was yelling at nobody. Mama only had her nightgown on too and her nipples were slipping out the side in a way that Shirley knew was not right when you were in the front yard.

But Shirley was relieved to see Mama so she ran as fast as she could to catch her and followed her through the front door. Just as she was about to catch up with Mama, Daddy grabbed her by the waist like she was a stick of firewood and ran outside with her again.

"Shirley, you've got to stay put," he yelled. But he didn't leave Shirley this time until Mama was back.

"Take Shirley and go get help. Mr. George and I'll get some buckets." And then he was gone, off toward the strange light of the house, and away from the darkness where Shirley shivered barefoot in the dew-wet grass.

Shirley knew what fire was. She knew fire from the Warm Morning Stove in the living room that kept them warm and from the wood cook range in the kitchen. Now her house was on fire. Then, as she stood there knowing that, the house caught fire everywhere, from side to side, from top to bottom. Her house was burning up. Her house was burning down.

Shirley remembered getting into the car with Mama to go for help, but nothing about their coming back. Her memory skipped like a fade-out on television, and then she was just standing there by Fannie watching the fire fill the sky clear up to the stars. Shirley's face was too hot from the heat of the fire, but her back was freezing, and her toes, digging in the May grass, were cold like ice cubes. That was the first time Shirley remembered her mind separating from her body. She was Shirley watching Shirley watch the house burn.

Daddy, and Gran Hudson, and C. C. Lee, and some others she couldn't name were passing buckets of water from the cistern to the house, but then they stopped.

"Might as well stand here and spit as much good as we're doing," Gran Hudson said. He looked all white and funny with no shirt on and no shoes, only his corduroy pants.

Then Daddy said, "The savings bonds."

Mama started saying over and over, "Don't, Dex. Don't." But Daddy was gone.

He couldn't get to the bond drawer, after all, but made a swipe at the closet. "Oh, Dex, your arm is burned," Mama said when he came running back to her.

All Daddy had managed to save were an armload of clothes that didn't fit anybody anymore, and the satin robe that Mama had worn on their wedding night. Daddy wrapped it around Mama's shoulders, and they laughed sort of sad like.

Then it was over. The house fell in with a crash, and Shirley stood there watching Shirley until there was nothing left of the house at all, until there were only bright red coals dancing on the ground.

Then Oriole Lee—Fannie's mom—said, "Come on home with us," and Fannie gave Shirley's hand a squeeze.

A Warm Morning

It isn't that I don't love the planet earth. I pick up trash on the side of the road and recycle glass, aluminum, paper and plastic with the best of them. I gave up aerosol deodorant twenty-five years ago. But when it comes to lowering the thermostat, I'm not made of the right stuff.

The truth is I have a Freudian fear of freezing to death that can be traced to the trauma of my early childhood. Born in the waning months of World War II, I came home from the hospital to Gran Hudson's Kentucky farmhouse. Although he owned over 800 acres of land and was considered well-to-do by local standards, he thought central heating was an extravagant luxury for town folks. He was not alone in that opinion. Looking back to the first dozen years of my life, I can't remember any home in our rural community that did not rely on a coal or wood-burning stove for winter warmth. Even the New Columbus School I attended through the sixth grade was heated by giant stoves towering in each of its three large classrooms. Despite the jumping and running that's inevitable when young children are cooped up inside in the wintertime with no place else to play, I don't recall any of my classmates ever falling against the stove and getting burned. From infancy, we had learned to behave when we got close to the fire that blazed, literally, in the middle of our living rooms.

At our house, a popular model incongruously called the "Warm Morning," dominated our lives. Tall and stout, this black creature met the dawn with a chilly stare unless it was fed and caressed like a colicky baby throughout the night. The plan,

41

always, was to stoke the fire well enough before bedtime so that it would smolder until morning. But often it would die out before daybreak despite Daddy's efforts. On those cold mornings, Daddy would have to reach into the bowels of the beast, seeking a hidden lever with one hand to shake down the ashes while gouging at its gut with a poker in his other hand. For reasons I did not understand, the ashes had to be vanquished before he could attempt to get a new fire up and going.

The ruins of yesterday's flames whirled through the early morning like a dust storm, choking the air and light out of the house, settling on the furniture, stifling our nostrils and our spirits. To me, it is the taste and smell of poverty. When I read of despair anywhere, the dry memories of those ashes settle in the back of my throat.

To escape, I would wrap myself, head and all, in Cousin Debbie Jones' hand sewn quilt—a housewarming gift to Mother after the old house burned down—and will Daddy to hurry, hurry, and get the nasty business done. But he couldn't rush the process, he said. It had to be done right, or the fire would falter again later in the day.

Closing off rooms to save on fuel is not a new idea, either. In my childhood home, and most everyone I knew did the same, we only attempted to heat three small rooms. The result was uneven. The living room, where the Warm Morning stood, was toasty warm, even blistering if you sat on the end of the sofa closest to the stove. The kitchen wasn't bad either because it got a boost from the electric range. The downstairs bedroom where my parents slept, however, was on the chilly side. The rest of the house—that would be the company dining room, a small hall that connected to the stairwell plus the entire upstairs—was shut off by a series of doors. Siberia could not have been colder.

Theoretically, my upstairs bedroom was warmer than the other closed off rooms because the chimney rose through it to escape through the roof. This made my parents feel better about my sleeping up there, I suppose, but only an Eskimo could have discerned any heat in the room. I would dress for bed downstairs, then open the door that sealed off the stairwell and sprint like an

Olympic runner up to my room under the eaves. I stopped for nothing until I reached the sanctuary beneath the bedcovers.

There I would lie, still, on the linen tundra, barely breathing. Inch by inch, I would claim more territory, sliding a toe, then a foot, then a leg across the frozen sheet. In the morning, the process would start over in reverse. It built character, I guess, to push my nose out from under the covers in a room where my breath hung in the air like smoke, but that was scant consolation.

The stove was a necessary evil, but Mother loathed it. She lived for the day in early spring when the sooty old thing could be taken down for the warm weather season and the doors to the rest of the house thrown open. The ugly, flowered linoleum, put down to protect the pretty wood floors from hot embers, would be rolled into storage too. It was like getting a new house.

But invariably Mother would take the stove down too early, and a Berry-Winter of some ilk would slam us. Then Daddy would grouse, "Are you trying to give us pneumonia?"

When I was thirteen, Mother returned to teaching. With the influence of her paycheck, she convinced Daddy to have Minch's Hardware in Owenton install an oil-burning furnace in our house. I viewed the new thermostat on the wall with the same awe that early man must have felt when he discovered fire. With the flick of a finger, I could have heat, all I wanted, even in my upstairs bedroom. I have lived joyfully in a hot house ever since.

Now, earnest and serious people I admire, chastise me at every turn for my extravagant wintertime consumption of fossil fuels, and my old joy is smudged with guilt. Some are frantic about global warming and the future of mankind, and I'm willing to listen, I'm receptive to alternative options—as long as I can stay really warm. Others, like my dear son-in-law Alex who prefers to keep their thermostat on sixty, are concerned about the cost of their monthly heating bill. I once pointed out to him that the Humane Society legally requires that the temperature in animal shelters be kept at sixty-five. We have reached an unspoken agreement. When I visit, he pretends not to notice that I inch the thermostat upward when no one is looking.

Still others, young and unfrozen, have re-discovered fuel-efficient stoves, and are as excited as if they'd invented the wheel. And heating only two or three rooms is a great idea, too, they add. I don't know whether to laugh or to cry. How can I explain to them that I'm still thawing out from my childhood? How do I describe the emotions that a cold house evokes in me? Because they're not logical, I know that. You can't explain dry memories of ashes in the back of your throat.

Mr. Stewart's Band

"What do you think of the glockenspiel?" he asked. As he waited for me to answer, he rubbed his chin with one hand while the other cradled his elbow. This was his serious stance not his more typical joking around mode.

To be honest, I didn't have a thought one about the glockenspiel. But I wanted to be in the band awful bad, so I said, "I think it sounds great. When's my first lesson?"

In addition to his work with band and choral music at the high school, Mr. Stewart traveled to the scattered elementary schools in the county teaching what I guess would be called music appreciation. Every other week, dull old arithmetic or geography would come to a halt and we grade schoolers would troop to the stage in our "gym-torium" for a 1950s version of fine arts class. He would play on the upright piano—oh, he was good—and we would sing songs like "Tell Me Why" and "On Top of Old Smokey" and "She'll Be Coming Around the Mountain" as loud as we could.

I loved singing, and I adored sweet, funny, handsome with a Cary-Grant-dimple-in-his-chin Mr. Stewart, but I couldn't carry a tune in the proverbial bucket. When the much ballyhooed seventh grade musical, *The Adventures of Tom Sawyer*, rolled around, I was cast in a small comic role. I wisely elected to pantomime the words in the chorus numbers.

It had become apparent to Mr. Stewart and me that despite my enthusiasm, the High School Glee Club was not in my future. It was about this time that he and I started talking about the possibility of my taking up a band instrument. We both saw the advantage of it. I wouldn't tilt the High School Glee Club off-key when I arrived as a freshman, and yet I'd still get to enjoy

45

music. After I thought about it, I decided band would be more fun than Glee Club anyway. The band got to go on trips to places like the State Fair in Louisville and the Tobacco Festival at Carrollton. And it played at every ballgame. Marching in formation to form a giant O C looked exciting.

In retrospect, I realize that Mr. Stewart may have suggested the glockenspiel because I could do little harm with it. It's an odd musical instrument, best described as a poor man's xylophone. At least in my hands, it never approached the resonant tones of its more uptown, swinging cousin. In lots of pieces, it has no part to play, and when it does come in, you can't hear it because of its loud neighbor, the bass drum.

The thing about Mr. Stewart is that he believed in giving everyone a chance, usually multiple chances as students tended to take advantage of his good nature and let him down. There was the time "music mice" ate up all the profit we might have made on the chocolate bars we were selling to buy new feathers for our caps. There was the time the seniors messed with the date of the regional contest on his calendar, and we got out of school and drove to Covington on the wrong day. There was the time— but I digress. The point is Mr. Stewart thought every student's education could be enriched by music.

Now in movies I've seen about music educators, the hard-nosed, no-nonsense teacher usually takes downtrodden, misfit children from the ghetto and drills them on how to play something like the violin until they end up so skillful they're invited to play at Carnegie Hall. Having learned to EXCEL the students are then able to whirl off to Juilliard—or at least to an engineering degree at MIT—without a backward glance at gangs, drugs and violent fathers.

Although we probably would have been classified as poor, disadvantaged farm kids if we'd had sense enough to know it, we never came close to excelling at music. In hindsight, I realize what an uphill struggle Mr. Stewart must have had organizing our countywide consolidated high school's first ever band. His budget was tiny, and it was almost impossible to gather scattered rural students for after school practice.

OCHS Band, 1961-1962 school year. First row, l-r: Lucy Baker, Gladys Kincaid, Verna Minch, Janet Thompson, Sandra Lewis, Grace Karen Hearne, Linda Butts, Lanny Cobb, Charles Arnold, Billy Elkins, Rita Suter. Second row, l-r: Gary Dunavent, Linda Sipple, Phyllis Ogden, Cookie Cull, Marc Cammack, Nancy Bray, Howard Olds, Andrew Cammack, Dan Sparrow, Jimmy Gibson, Scott Noel. Standing, l-r: Marvin Stewart, Betsy Ross Ford, Kenny Haydon, Johnny Wilson, Donna Cohorn, Georgia Green.

So in spite of Mr. Stewart's talent and encouragement, our band was ragged. When we marched, our bass drummer, a laid back, affable fellow, was habitually out of step. Our lines were crooked despite the drum major's loudest efforts. Our OC wobbled around and ended up looking more like a D trailed by an O with a small bite out of it. The clarinets were forever bringing practice to a screeching halt with their broken reeds. Our ace trumpet player—who actually was quite good—would periodically shout, "We stink!" and go on strike for the rest of the week. Some days, not all sections ended at the same time, on the same note—

None of this seemed to get to Mr. Stewart. He went right on laughing, telling jokes, encouraging us, and introducing new music. He pushed us out there at ballgames, to parades and competitions and at least once a year into a joint concert with other neighboring high schools with a big deal guest conductor. He seemed to believe there was joy in the doing, in the making of music, even mediocre music. That was an important lesson for this over earnest student to learn.

I had one big number, "Stars and Stripes Forever," where the glockenspiel had a one measure solo. As the old Sousa march swelled to a crescendo, I would tense with anticipation. Then he'd nod his head towards me, and smile, and I would hit the bells with all the force I had—too loud, I realize now. But for thirty seconds, I made music large enough, grand enough, to burst my heart.

One after another, we graduated, and became teachers, farmers, businessmen. Our saxophonist became one of the preeminent ministers in the Southeast. But none of us went on to careers in music that I know of. Certainly, Mr. Stewart did not make a musician out of me.

But we did make music once. Music joyful enough, forgiving enough, to burst our hearts.

Elvis and Me

Elvis may have left the building, but he hasn't left me. I never outgrew him. I never saw the need.

I wish I could remember the first time I heard him sing on the radio, wish I could say that I knew at that moment a star was born. But I was a child in grade school when his songs began to blow the top off the music charts, and I suspect I only started paying attention after I heard other kids talking about him.

My pal Judy Parr was almost always the first in our crowd to hear his newest record. Her family listened to the radio while they ate breakfast. Mine, on the other hand, kept TV's "Today" show blaring in the morning, which gave me a distinct disadvantage. In an effort to scoop Judy, I started turning the volume on my radio down low in my upstairs bedroom so my parents couldn't hear it in theirs downstairs, and left it playing all night. Sometimes, waking briefly at one or two in the morning, I'd catch the strains of a new title, and sigh in anticipation of a schoolyard triumph.

The next day, feigning nonchalance, I would ask, "Have you heard Elvis' latest song?" I'd hold my breath until her answer came. I've never felt cooler than I did on those long-ago recess breaks when she would occasionally answer, "No, what's it called?"

I was never cool again when it came to pop music. The Beatles hit the world like a tsunami about the time I finished high school and entered college, but I didn't have time for them. They looked like skinny boys with bad haircuts to me and, over serious, I was busy getting to where I intended to go. I also took a little detour into folk music in college, and apparently it was the wrong turn to take. Nobody talks about Peter, Paul and Mary

49

much anymore, but the Beatles are everywhere. I've always understood there was something about the Beatles I didn't get that the rest of the world does. Sure, I thought the rhythm of their music was good for dancing, and the melded sound of their voices was pleasing. Occasionally a lyric would hang in my head, but they didn't have the soul, and—I'll say it—the sexuality that Elvis' voice did.

A lot has been written about the outrage his rock and rolling hips caused among the aging gatekeepers of pop culture. But you know, most of us never saw Elvis wiggle, at least not until long after we'd fallen in love with him, and his movies hit the local drive-in theater. No, the sensuousness was all there in his radio voice from the beginning. A girl would have had to be deaf—or dead—not to hear it. It was bad, it was wonderful, and it told me everything I wanted to know but was afraid to ask.

I think, too, people like Judy Parr and me intuitively knew that he was one of us. He was a southern kid with country roots who probably knew as much as we did about staring down spiders in outhouses and singing hymns in church on Sunday mornings.

So no, I never outgrew Elvis. In his later years, though, I longed to help him. I read about his boredom, his desire to expand his mind as he dabbled in the paranormal, went spying for President Nixon, and other foolishness. By then I was a grown married woman teaching school. I began to think maybe if I could pull him into my high school English class I could save him through literature. Elvis had the soul of a reader, I always thought, if he'd had the right sort of teacher. I know it's a stretch to picture Elvis settling into a chair in my monthly book club, but he'd done so much for me, it seemed little enough for me to do in return.

Now, as Lewis Grizzard said, Elvis is dead, and I don't feel so good myself. I wish I could write him a fan letter, something I never did when he was alive.

"Thank you," I'd say. "Thank you. Thank you very much."

Bubby

Bubby passed away at 5:30 a.m., Verna wrote in her email. I stopped reading, and sat quiet for a while remembering. Time enough to learn about "arrangements" later.

But I had to smile. We both thought of this gentle giant—this man whose life had impacted thousands, perhaps indirectly millions—as "Bubby." Certainly, Bubby was no Bubba.

I never asked anyone how he got his nickname. It's just what we called him all through school even as he grew very tall and handsome and his voice deepened into a booming resonance.

Bubby's family and my father's both had roots that reached back to Brushy Creek. In the way of Owen County—and of other rural sections of Kentucky—our people had known and respected each other for generations. My first personal memories of Bubby, though, date to middle school when we kept running into each other at sub-district MYF (Methodist Youth Fellowship) functions. He and I belonged to the Methodist minority in a county where Baptists prevailed, and that uniqueness was a bond.

Years later, he would talk about those MYF meetings, and tell me how he gripped the back of the pew until his knuckles were white. That's how hard he resisted the call he felt to the ministry, he said. Like Jonah, he didn't want to do it, and I can understand that. On a personal level, the ministry requires sacrifice. With Bubby's sharp mind and easy way with people, he could have been successful at most anything. He could have become a wealthy man.

As freshmen, Bubby and I became classmates at consolidated Owen County High, and we both signed up for a four-year stint with Mr. Stewart's band. I was along for the ride, faking it with the glockenspiel so I could go on the band's trips to the state fair and such. But Bubby was an excellent saxophone player. To this day, the saxophone remains my favorite instrument, and I think that's because I watched Bubby, always a row in front of me, smoothing the jagged edges of band practice with his sax's mellow sound.

Had it not been for Sandy, I might have set my cap for him. But Sandy laid claim on him in grade school, and she was so beautiful, so perfect for him, no one else had much of a chance. From time to time, however, he would get a restless eye as teenage boys will do, and then Sandy would come and sit by me on the band trip bus. I would listen and advise patience. I was no Dear Abby, but I was confident of my advice because I'd noticed that she rarely had to be patient for long.

We elected Bubby president of our senior class, and got a glimpse of who he would become as he led us through our various ceremonies with uncommon grace. On graduation night, he and I walked side by side down the aisle to the strains of "Pomp and Circumstance"—for no reason I recall other than his being the tallest boy and my being the tallest girl in the Class of '63.

I don't know when Bubby stopped resisting God's polite request to preach. He didn't casually talk about it at school. He was not sanctimonious. He cut up like everybody else, though he was never mean spirited or wild. But not long after entering college, when he was eighteen, he preached his first sermon to his first tiny church.

When Ernie and I married the summer after we graduated from college, we asked Bubby to officiate. He didn't tell us until years later that ours was the first wedding he'd performed by himself. Not yet fully ordained, he had sought special permission from his Bishop. Forty-one years later, we're still together—and it tickled Bubby that his first wedding "took."

Life carried us to different parts of the country, and we saw each other infrequently in the decades that followed. Active in our local Methodist Church, however, we kept up with Bubby's ministry. Each church he was assigned flourished under his leadership. Perhaps this was because he spent fifteen hours preparing every 20-minute sermon he preached. Perhaps this was because of the new ideas he was willing to try, or his insistence on "loving one another radically." Perhaps this was because he never forgot to minister to individuals.

When my mother moved to Lexington after Daddy's death, she was in a fragile state. I hadn't seen Bubby in years, but I called and left a message at his Lexington church office asking him to call her if he had time. I never heard back from him—but Mother did. The next day he showed up at her strange new apartment, never telling her that I'd called, and talked with her for an hour or two. "There's nothing like people from home," she told me on our daily long distance call that night. It was a turning point in her grief.

About eleven years ago, Bubby was hit by lymphoma. He fought it into remission three times, never slowing up on his life's work. Sometime during this period, he was assigned to Brentwood United Methodist Church in Nashville. During his ministry there, the membership grew to 7000.

Longtime Kentucky friends of ours, Helen and Carroll Wood, were among those new members. When we visited a few years ago, we attended services together at Brentwood. With a full head of snow-white hair, and towering in his clerical robes, Bubby looked like a figure Michelangelo might have painted. I was somewhat awestruck at the grandness of the church, too. As Bubby joked, his high pulpit alone was larger than some of the Kentucky churches he'd preached in.

But when he began to speak in his powerful voice, I felt as though he were talking only to me. The people laughed, the people wept. The rafters trembled. And I understood why God had been so persistent in calling Bubby to preach.

Last year, colon cancer hit Bubby, and this time there would be no remission despite his daily conversations with God about the subject. Yet disease didn't stop him. He wrote yet another book—this time a best-seller co-authored with the retired CEO of Dollar General Stores. He continued to preach every Sunday, in fact, until three weeks ago. The title of his last sermon was—"Don't Stop."

The Reverend Doctor J. Howard Olds, 62, died June 23, 2008. Sandy and the boys were with him. But I have a feeling death won't stop him.

My Hat

This week an old friend who lives on the other side of the continent dropped back into my life. We were classmates and sorority sisters during our college days at Transylvania College (now University), but we haven't seen each other in over forty years.

Reunions are as sweet as ripe fall pears when you've reached our stage of life. We've talked non-stop about the old days, the new days, and many of the ones in between.

But we haven't talked about the wide-brimmed felt hat I wore to the Freshman Tea. Because I can't, even now, do so without blushing.

The early sixties were a confusing time to come of age, especially in Kentucky. (Mark Twain, you may recall, said he wanted to die in Kentucky because everything happens ten years later here than in the rest of the country.) Time magazine was running cover stories about the sexual revolution on America's college campuses, psychedelic drug use, and student sit-ins for civil rights in the south.

My college handbook, on the other hand, told me in no uncertain terms that I was expected to wear a skirt, never slacks, to class, and that all Transylvania students were expected to "dress for dinner" each evening in the college dining hall. That meant high heels and a nice dress for coeds, jackets and ties for males.

The handbook was mailed to my home weeks before classes began, and I crammed so that I wouldn't break any of the many rules. Freshmen were to be in their rooms studying from eight until ten each weeknight. Lights were to be turned out at eleven. Even an upperclass woman had to sign out and state her destination whenever she left the dorm after six p.m. Of course there

54

was a strict curfew, nine during the week and midnight on Friday and Saturday nights. And if a boy were ever caught in a co-ed's dorm room—well, the handbook didn't spell out the punishment but I inferred she would be drawn and quartered by the Dean of Women on the lawn of Old Morrison Chapel.

We freshmen arrived on campus on a hot September Sunday, and our first official event was a late afternoon tea at the college President's home. Growing up on a tobacco farm at Natlee, I'd always taken my tea with ice in a tall glass usually slouched on the front porch glider. But I understood that "a tea" was not about what we'd be drinking. I'd been in a small tizzy over what to wear.

Mother, however, assured me she knew what one wore to a tea at the President's house. She'd attended college in the early 1940s, and knew about such things. A nice day dress would be appropriate, but of course, I'd have to co-ordinate a matching hat. "One always wears a hat to a tea," she said. Having seen all those photographs of Queen Elizabeth in *Life* magazine, I knew she was right.

So off we went to purchase my debut college outfit at the best store we could think of, Wolf Wiles Department Store down in Lexington. Stores like Wolf Wiles don't exist in the suburban shopping mall world that most Americans know today. It was a little like the better Manhattan stores I've ambled through in later years, quiet and elegant, except the clerks weren't arrogant. It might be better compared to a contemporary boutique except it was huge, rambling over multiple, long, wide floors plus a mezzanine. The faint scent of expensive perfume permeated its every nook.

I settled on a fitted, navy sheath dress with discreet red piping in just the right places. I have to say that in my memory it was one of the more flattering dresses I ever owned. Then it was time to select the hat.

I felt like Cinderella dressing for the ball when I sat down in one of the satin chairs in front of a long bank of mirrors in the hat department. The kind saleswoman brought one headpiece after another for me try. Finally, she and Mother and even several passers-by agreed that the simple, unembellished—but large—navy felt hat was perfect for my height (tall) and for my dress (straight and narrow.) With its wide brim dipping asymmetrically to the top of one eyebrow, the hat was sophisticated and chic. I never felt as glamorous, before or since, as I did the moment I decided to buy that hat.

Georgia at Transylvania College

You have guessed how this story ends. I was the only girl at the Freshman Tea who wore a hat. Standing at least 5'10" or more in my heels and dramatic headgear, I was not even able to fade into the shadows.

Lest you think I'm exaggerating my *faux pas*, let me share that decades later classmates at reunions would make remarks about their first impression of me, saying they had thought I was a professor "in my hat." Apparently, everyone who was at the tea remembers my hat. And not in a good way, though I think I probably did look good. I was out of step when blending in was the assignment we'd been given that afternoon.

I wish I could say that I laughed off the incident, that I was indifferent to being different. But I was mortified, perhaps as much for Mother as for myself. I'd never known her to be dead-wrong before. Despite her intelligence and wisdom, I had arrived in this new cosmopolitan world I was entering looking like a country bumpkin who was trying too hard.

Off balance, I continued to make missteps that fall, and I never again was the self-assured girl I'd been in my small high school. I've often regretted the confident edge I lost that first afternoon at college, and wondered if my life would have turned out ever so altered if I hadn't worn a hat to the Freshman Tea.

Yet it may have been good to learn at the outset how very much I had to learn. After forty years, I've concluded that grasping the scope of one's ignorance is about what a college education amounts to.

Omar Carr's Thanksgiving

Omar Carr walked out of the Old Testament and down the aisle of the New Columbus Methodist Church to lay the fruits of his labor on God's altar. He didn't wear flowing robes like Abraham and Elijah and the others I'd seen in pictures. He favored denim overalls, and his thick reddish brown hair was held in place with a weathered felt brimmed hat, but he had the look of a patriarch nonetheless. Even a child could tell that Omar's offering was what Cain should have been about instead of goofing off and picking fights with his brother Abel.

Each November Mr. Carr transformed our plain little country church into a della Robbia masterpiece. Our simple oak altar rail, hand varnished by someone in the 19th century, stretched in a wide oval from near one front corner of the church on the left, to near the other front corner on the right. Its simplicity was beautiful in all seasons, but at Thanksgiving, embellished with the profusion of Mr. Carr's homegrown fruit and vegetables, it rivaled the splendor of Italian cathedrals.

Now I'm not talking about a few corn shucks and pumpkins scattered around that even the likes of me could muster. Mr. Carr—who had the blue ribbons to prove it—grew the finest array of vegetables and fruit in the state of Kentucky and his presentation at our church was an artistic creation. Squashes and gourds of all size and variety, in every hue of the rainbow, dense multi-dimensional layers, high and then low, of apples, pears, eggplant, potatoes, and corn in exotic colors, oh the list goes on—adorned and engulfed the altar rail, filling up the front of the church as though a cornucopia in Heaven were overflowing and raining down upon us.

In the 1950s—perhaps even now—the Methodist Church promoted a program called the "Lord's Acre" in rural areas. Farm people were encouraged to donate the proceeds generated by one acre of land and the money was then used for a specific outreach such as Methodist orphanages or inner city and foreign missions. At our small church, the Lord's Acre offerings were laid on the altar during a ceremony that followed the annual Thanksgiving dinner held on a November Wednesday night. To be honest, I think most people just gave what they wanted to or what they could. But in Omar Carr's case, it appeared he had taken the injunction literally and carried in the bounty of an entire acre—probably more—to underscore the symbolism of our endeavor.

For as long as anyone could remember, Mr. Carr had grown the best vegetables and fruits around and entered them in competition at the Kentucky State Fair. He won in nearly every category he entered and was a perennial "Best of Show." In fact, he amassed so many grand championship ribbons, his wife had more than enough to piece an heirloom quilt for the family.

No one else in our off-the-beaten-track community entered the agricultural competitions at the state fair in Louisville. I don't remember others even growing gardens as diverse as his. Most grew only some tomatoes and beans, and perhaps some cushaw, a popular variety of squash in Owen County at that time, and a little corn for roasting ears in the summer. A few grew potatoes. Tobacco—the cash crop in the region—absorbed most everyone's time and energy and restrained their enthusiasm for gardening.

But Mr. Carr grew everything he could coax from his Owen County hills. He was a man of few words, and so his family doesn't know why or how he was motivated to become such a master gardener. Nor do they recall why he began showing his produce at the state fair. Perhaps a county extension agent encouraged him. Perhaps he just "took a notion." What they do recall is that the state fair became a multi-generational excursion, an annual and treasured camping trip for his large family, children and grandchildren alike, who slept in the barns with other exhibiters, and helped Omar carry and tinker with his displays until no one else had a chance at claiming the blue

59

ribbons. His *tour de force* at the Kentucky exhibition extended for thirty years, from the early 1930s until his death in 1964. He died in August of that year only minutes after leaving his garden where he had been prepping his crop for the soon to open fair.

One year, I attended the state fair myself to participate in the 4-H speech contest. I decided to look up Mr. Carr's exhibits over in the far exposition hall. They were wonderful, of course, and he was, once again, the overall winner. But somehow, they didn't look as magnificent to me as the dramatic panorama he created for our church family each November. I wondered then if Mr. Carr gave his finest effort to us.

What I know is this. Though I was but a child, Mr. Carr helped me understand the generosity of the earth and of God in a way that transcended language, with a beauty that required no words. With his hoe and with his art, he affirmed the abundance of life itself, and led my young heart—and yet does now—to prayer in thanksgiving.

The Kentucky River

Here in Kentucky ... [the] past has always felt close and I've always felt connected to it, sprung from it, like it or not. Down the road from my house is an old family graveyard. One of the graves there is for a woman whose first name was America. Even though I live in the middle of nowhere, sometimes it feels like I live in the center of it all.
— Poet Maurice Manning, *Southeast Review*, 2008

Long before caravans of diesel trucks crisscrossed the nation on the interstate highway system. Long before the railroads pushed freight across America from sea to shining sea. Before the Chicago commodities exchange. Before Dow Jones became a household name. Before any of that—there were the rivers carved out by God.

The mighty Ohio forms near Pittsburgh and with its many tributaries sweeps westward until it eventually empties into the wide Mississippi at Cairo, Illinois, a few miles from Paducah in far western Kentucky. In turn, the Mississippi rushes southward with its co-mingled waters to the port of New Orleans. Thus, fledgling America had a natural superhighway that stretched almost 2000 miles from the northeast corridor to the Gulf of Mexico.

And that made all the difference. Without the rivers to move cargo from producers to markets in the 18th and 19th centuries, America might have remained a small, skinny country hunkered along the Atlantic seaboard. The rivers—and the men who navigated them—are central to America's story of westward expansion, and their role in developing the young nation's abundant economy cannot be overstated.

61

Here in Kentucky—America's first western frontier—the Ohio River and its tributaries defined who we would become, determined where we would build our towns, and enabled us to get our agricultural products to a world market. The Ohio, of course, jigsaws Kentucky's northern boundary east to west, and lies, interestingly enough, within Kentucky—not in the state of Ohio. But the state's smaller Kentucky River also has played a significant role in American commerce.

The Kentucky River rambles 259 miles, commencing in the mountains of eastern Kentucky, then cutting through the lush bluegrass region of the state creating limestone palisades that are the stuff of poetry, before leveling out and flowing through flat fertile valleys on its journey to the sea. Forty miles of the lower Kentucky River pass through my particular place on earth, Owen County, not long before the river empties into the Ohio at Carrollton near Louisville.

As early as 1787—only twelve years after Daniel Boone established Boonesborough in the western wilderness—Kentucky agriculture products exceeded the demands of local markets. Pork, flour and tobacco were going to waste in storage. The market that was needed in those early days was New Orleans which unfortunately was under the control of Spain.

In 1789, when negotiations with Spain finally opened the markets in New Orleans to Americans, historian Dr. Thomas Clark says the Kentucky River quickly became "lined with boats on their way to New Orleans." These were still powerless flatboats, but thus began transportation of farm products on the Kentucky.

In Owen County, this early river traffic resulted in warehouses being built at locations such as Gratz and Monterey, and these became the natural points in later decades for steamboats to pick up cargo to be carried to Louisville and Cincinnati and points beyond. By mid-19th century, cities along the Ohio had become primary markets, but often the steamboats hurried cargo right on to New Orleans, which could be reached in 12 days if all went well.

Owen Countians of all types engaged in this chain of commerce. My g-grandfather, Amos Noel, was an independent tobacco buyer at Monterey, purchasing tobacco directly from farmers in the barn and shipping it on to market by steamboat from the Monterey warehouse and dock.

Others engaged with the river itself. Navigators straight out of a Mark Twain novel, they knew the bowels of the Kentucky River as intimately as a surgeon knows the human body.

The Falls City II at the Gratz Wharf

Noble Nash Hundley, a resident of Gratz, was one of Owen County's most notable river men. Noble Nash—like Mark Twain—was a steamboat pilot. He piloted a number of boats in his lifetime, but was fondest of the time he spent on the grand Falls City II, a familiar steamboat on the Kentucky, the Ohio, and the Mississippi in the years from 1898 to about 1915. His granddaughter, Owenton resident Sandra Hundley Stafford, has a drawing hanging in her home that pictures her grandfather standing on the Falls City II.

In *The Kentucky River*, historian William E. Ellis writes that it "was the premier boat on the Kentucky River at the turn of the century." He goes on to describe its vast size, noting that it had "an elevator to carry 90 hogsheads of tobacco to the hold with the ability to haul 100 more on its deck." It also transported all kinds of livestock to market. Remarkably, it also had room for passengers. Since it was the only way to go, the rich and the poor, the famous and the infamous, rode the Falls City II together. It cost about six or seven dollars, including meals, for overnight accommodations from Frankfort to Louisville. Special holiday excursions featured dancing on the deck. Often the Falls City II carried traveling shows that performed at small river towns like Monterey and Gratz. (Ellis, 26.)

As might be expected of a steamboat pilot, Noble Nash Hundley was a handsome man, a weathered Clark Gable type straight out of central casting. He was born in 1863 in Port Royal, the son of Evan Hundley and Elizabeth Wilson Hundley. He married Laura Douthitt, 24 February, 1891, in Henry County, and if family lore can be believed, he pampered her like a princess. According to her granddaughter, the beautiful Laura would dress in her corsets and finery every day, and then sit fanning on her porch watching for Noble Nash's return on the river.

Noble Nash's sister, Pearl Hawkins, also watched for him. She lived near the Kentucky River in Henry County, and often he would stop and spend a night at her house. To let her know he was coming, he'd send up a special signal with the steamboat's whistle.

The family tells other stories about Noble Nash. The one I like best occurred in the winter of 1917-18 when the rivers froze over solid leaving him stranded in Carrollton. Determined to get home to Laura and the children, he bought a pair of ice skates and skated 25 miles on the frozen Kentucky to reach his hearth at Gratz.

In his history of the river, Ellis tells this story in which Hundley is an unnamed but certain player. "Steamboats often raced, illegally, and not just for sport," he writes. In one such race, the steamboat Rescue beat The Falls City II through the lock at Monterey. Not to be outdone in the competition for freight revenue, the wily Falls City II "dispatched its deck hands overland to tobacco warehouses at Gratz. When the Rescue arrived in Gratz the Falls City's workmen had commandeered the town and were already emptying the tobacco warehouse in anticipation of their boat's arrival." (Ellis, 26.)

In time, of course, the steamboats gave way to the railroads which could move freight faster and cheaper and to more places. The dashing river men like Noble Nash Hundley faded into folklore and legend.

But the rivers that spawned them endure.

A Bit of America's Story

Writing is a lonely avocation. I'm reminded of the old movie where Jimmy Stewart rambles on to Harvey, a giant white rabbit no one can see or hear. I write, caught up in a one-sided conversation with readers who are as invisible as Stewart's Harvey, and wonder if they may have left the room without a sound.

So when the phone rang a few weeks ago, I was delighted to learn that my essay about the Kentucky River had resonated with the caller, Mr. Charles Clements, of Louisville. Mr. Clements, age 82, was especially moved by poet Maurice Manning's words that I'd quoted in the preamble. I told him he had a discerning ear. Manning was a finalist for the Pulitzer Prize in poetry last year, and is one of America's preeminent poets. He calls Kentucky home.

Manning had written, "Down the road from my house is an old family graveyard. One of the graves there is for a woman whose first name was America." Digging through old census records in my genealogy research, I've learned to my surprise and delight that America was a relatively popular name for women in the early 19th century. Mr. Clements, however, had heard of none other than his great-grandmother who bore that astonishing name. His voice was edged with emotion as he told me that his America—America Rowlett—was also buried in a family cemetery, but one that lies in Owen County near the Kentucky River. And then Mr. Clements proceeded to tell me in his own words, eloquent in their simplicity, but echoing Mannings', that the "past has always felt close and I've always felt connected to it, sprung from it, like it or not."

With a Revolutionary War veteran's land grant in hand, his grandmother's people, the Rowletts, arrived in what would later become Owen County, Kentucky, by at least 1790—earlier if family lore is accurate. They settled where Severn Creek flows into the Kentucky River at a spot still known locally as Rowlett's Landing. The lower Kentucky flows in the shape of a giant oxbow through that region, curling around a wide fertile valley named "Clements Bottom" on modern day maps of the region. Rowlett's Landing lies near the center of the bow, about halfway between the present-day communities of Monterey and Gratz. One generation or another of Mr. Clements's family has owned that place on earth for over two hundred years. He took owner-ship of it in 1976, and now it has passed to his son.

Stories about his people and the land they called home were as common to his childhood as fairy tales. The earliest settlers, for example, had found limestone covered mounds scattered throughout the Severn Creek valley. These are thought to have been cremation sites configured by Native Americans of the ancient Adena culture who wandered the area between 1000 to 200 BC. The stones had been moved by his time, but in childish irreverence, he bounded to the top of the mounds and down, time and again.

His family also spoke of a mysterious limestone watchtower that once stood on a hill south of Severn Creek. It, too, is believed to have been built by the Adena people. Like the white men who came after them more than two thousand years later, the Adena employed the Kentucky River for travel and trade. It's likely that the point now called Rowlett's Landing was once part of the Adena's extensive trading network that stretched from the Great Lakes to the Gulf Coast.

Mr. Clements's early Kentucky ancestors established a trad-ing post at Rowlett's Landing. In flatboat days, all matter of farm products were shipped from there to New Orleans. Oral tradition says they were often paid in Spanish dollars back then which were cut into pieces called "bits" when small change was needed.

Later, when steamboats began to plow the river, the trading post morphed into a general store that served the community, and a warehouse was established nearby where freight such as tobacco could be stored for pick-up by a passing steamboat. A large wooden screw was used to compress the tobacco into hogsheads for shipping on to Louisville markets, and Mr. Clements's family still has that apparatus.

Then—my cup runneth over—another reader called who had read the essay about the Kentucky River. Joyce Hardin, of Springfield, reported that her husband's late grandfather, W. D. Hardin, of Monterey, and his brother, Thomas Hardin, were among the owners of the Louisville and Kentucky River Packet Company which owned two steamboats that carried the name Falls City. The one pictured in the newspaper with my story was the later of the two, built about 1898, and is known by historians as the Falls City II.[*] However, each steamboat during its period of service, she says, was referred to in the vernacular and on its signage as simply the "Falls City."[**]

Her family retains the Falls City logbooks detailing the pick-ups and sales at stops such as Hardin's Landing, Monterey, Rowlett's Landing, and Gratz. Kentucky-American Water Company, in recognition of the Hardin family's role in local river history, has named its large, new facility in Owen County, "Hardin's Landing Water Treatment Plant."

Her call sent me on a quest for more information. I now know more about steamboats with Falls City in their name than any woman prone to seasickness should. There were at least five, and Mark Twain, himself, piloted one of them—called "The

---

[*] Kentucky historian William E. Ellis writes, "The Falls City II was the premier boat on the Kentucky ... from 1898—1908." Following a shift to the Mississippi River, he reports that it was scrapped in 1915. William E. Ellis, *The Kentucky River* (Univ Press of Kentucky: Lexington, 2000) 26.

[**] My research in early newspaper articles is consistent with Joyce Hardin's understanding that the various reincarnations of the Falls City steamboat on the Kentucky River were each called simply the "Falls City" by contemporaries, and not "Falls City II" etc. Each also displayed only the name "Falls City." This has caused confusion for many when attempting to identify the year/years a particular photograph was taken. However, the photograph of the Falls City II included here was likely taken about 1905.

New Falls City"—on the Mississippi. Maybe I'll expand on that topic another day.

For now, I will only say that I am ever amazed at how grounded Kentuckians are in their local history, how deep and rich their sense of place remains even into the 21st century, how tenderly they treasure the stories of their people. America Rowlett—or America Smith or Jones—we are, indeed, each of us, a bit of America's story, "connected to it, sprung from it, like it or not."

Carl Johnson

I was sixteen years old when Carl Johnson died on this ribbon of a road that winds between the river and a limestone cliff. He was not much older. We never spoke a word to each other. At least, I have no memory of his voice. But his black eyes looked out on the world through long, angel lashes and all the girls agreed that he was beautiful. If you favored delicate-boned, olive skinned boys, that is, which I didn't, preferring taller, studier types. Still, he glided through the hallways of the school, thin and lithe, elegant in crisp oxford cloth and khaki, anticipating life, getting ready, like I was, until one day he wasn't.

For ten years, twenty years, now almost fifty, I slow as I enter the curve on the river road where he crashed into the wall of rock.

"This is where Carl Johnson died," I say as I always do, as if this were an important historical fact.

It is not, I suppose. Although he was never late for geometry class, he didn't live long enough to do much but be a boy. He did, however, comb his shining black hair neatly to the left. Or maybe he brushed it upward into a flattop, a trendy style that year. What I do remember is that his hair sparkled in the light and that it was always as perfect as a picture in a magazine.

And so if I could—were it left up to me—I'd plant one of those fancy iron markers at this turn in the highway, the kind that has words so tiny and dense you can't read them as you whiz by in your car, but it lets you know in no uncertain terms that you're passing a significant place.

"HERE," it would say, "halfway between the once thriving villages of Monterey and Gratz at a bend in the lower Kentucky River so beautiful the artist Paul Sawyier might have paused one morning in the nineteen-oughts to paint its green blue water wide and deep as it rushes to merge with the Ohio thirty miles downstream, HERE beside the broad river bottom where cattle graze on burial mounds hallowed by the Adena peoples, HERE where ice and time shoved a limestone hill a hundred feet straight up from the ground and then rolled out a long valley to rest beside it—HERE the immortality of Georgia's youth hit the ditch on a June evening so sweet you could taste it."

After half a century, though, only weeds push their way through the stone to mark the spot. The river flows on past the mounds built by ancient people, in a hurry to reach its destination, an ocean or maybe a polar cap.

And so I slow as I enter the curve on the river road where he crashed into the wall of rock.

"This is where Carl Johnson died," I say as I always do, as if this were an important historical fact.

Where We're From

As far as we can tell, Nancy and I aren't kin, not even a smidgen. However, my cousin's grandmother—that would be Uncle Ed Hudson's wife who was a Davis—is her great-aunt. Thus, in the exacting way of computers, her Google quest for roots led her to my Hudson Family tree posted on the Internet.

In the email conversations that followed over the next few months, I learned that California had pulled her maternal grandparents away from their native Owen County in the 1930s. The Depression era was a turbulent period in America's history, and many people, like Nancy's family, found their way to California where sunshine and possibilities beckoned.

She, herself, has lived all her life in the golden state and knew little to nothing about her mother's people. Now that retirement has given her time for research, she's set out, armed with a few hand-me-down stories, to learn as we say in Kentucky, where she's from.

In Nancy's case, I was able to tell her that she's from southeastern Owen County where her Davis, True, and Holbrook ancestors settled in the late 18th century. Given their involvement with the Mountain Island and Mussel Shoals Churches, some of them likely arrived in the wilderness on foot by way of the Cumberland Gap with The Rev. Elijah Craig and his independent band of Baptists called "The Traveling Church." This was a group of five to six hundred free-minded people who set off from Spotsylvania County, Virginia, in early 1781 to escape the tyranny of England's Anglican Church.[*]

---

[*] Ranck, George W. *The Traveling Church*. Louisville: Press of Baptist Book Concern, 1891.

When Nancy's grandparents headed further west in the 1930s, they left behind 140 plus years of family history in Kentucky, enough time, I assured her, for us to claim her as one of our own. To her surprise, she has a slew of distant relatives still living in the area since many folks around here trace their ancestry back to the same families as she does.

Recently, Ernie and I and my Hudson cousins Emily and Ed (who are kin to Nancy on the other side of their family tree) had the pleasure of meeting her and her son and daughter-in-law. It was their first visit to Kentucky, and seeing our springtime lushness and the beauty of our land through their new eyes, I was proud of my place.

They wanted to scour cemeteries, an obsession with gene-alogists, for old tombstones and missing information, and we were pleased to guide them. Our first stop was on Rt. 1739 near Lusby's Mill and Eagle Creek at the Mussel Shoals Baptist Church, which is surrounded by an ancient graveyard. It's a quaint, tranquil place straight out of a pastoral painting or a movie set, but it's also a sacred spot significant in the religious history and culture of the region.

Mussel Shoals—still open for God's business—was founded in 1817 by members who had been dismissed for that purpose and with blessings from the Mountain Island Baptist Church upstream on Eagle Creek. The older church on Mountain Island (est. July 13, 1801—disbanded in the 1930s) had in turn been established by members from Elijah Craig's Great Crossings Church.[**] Most historians include Mountain Island among the original Traveling Church congregations because it was founded by elders who traveled into the Kentucky territory with the Craigs.

And so we walked the old Mussel Shoals Cemetery sur-rounded by this history. The look on Nancy's face, part joy, part amazement, when she found the graves of her g-g-grandparents was a poem as moving as any I've read in a book.

As we parted with promises to keep in touch, I was left to wonder what motivates people to travel 2000 miles to stare at

---

[**] Bryant, James C. *Mountain Island In Owen County, Kentucky: The Settlers and Their Churches.* Owenton: Owen Hist Soc, 1986.

toppled-over tombstones surrounded by hayfields? What is it that drives us to define where we're from?

I'm not sure. But I do know that where we're from is a complicated place, more than geography, though that's part of the answer. It's more than names on a chart, too, though we may count the generations backward to infinity.

In her iconic poem, "Where I'm From," Kentucky writer George Ella Lyon shapes a provocative response to that familiar question. Teachers across America, in China and Ecuador, have used her words to help others arrive at their own answer. Ms. Lyon has graciously given me permission to reprint her poem here. And so, I ask—where are you from?

Where I'm From

by George Ella Lyon

I am from clothespins,
from Clorox and carbon-tetrachloride.
I am from the dirt under the back porch.
(Black, glistening,
it tasted like beets.)
I am from the forsythia bush
the Dutch elm
whose long-gone limbs I remember
as if they were my own.

I'm from fudge and eyeglasses,
from Imogene and Alafair.

I'm from the know-it-alls
and the pass-it-ons,
from Perk up! and Pipe down!
I'm from He restoreth my soul
with a cottonball lamb
and ten verses I can say myself.

I'm from Artemus and Billie's Branch,
fried corn and strong coffee.

Georgia Green Stamper

From the finger my grandfather lost
to the auger,
the eye my father shut to keep his sight.

Under my bed was a dress box
spilling old pictures,
a sift of lost faces
to drift beneath my dreams.
I am from those moments—
snapped before I budded—
leaf-fall from the family tree.

"Where I'm From" is reprinted by permission of the author

You Might As Well Laugh

prologue ii …

you might as well laugh Mother always said

Humor is … a sense of intellectual perspective: an awareness
that some things are really important, others not; and that the
two kinds are most oddly jumbled in everyday affairs.
— Christopher Morley

I can count on my fingers the times I saw Mother cry, but she
laughed most every day. She was not a funny person, however. She didn't have Daddy's wit, that perfect quip at the right
moment, or his comedic gift for telling a story that could make
you laugh until your side ached. But she had a humorist's
perspective on life, a dead-on instinct for sorting Morley's
"really important" stuff from the "not." When things went awry
but the worst didn't happen, she'd say, "You might as well
laugh." When far-sighted Aunt Sis accidentally made her famous
pink potato salad with oven degreaser instead of salad oil—and
we didn't end up in the hospital. When my high school buddy,
Sally, broke her leg in a car accident en route to buy shoes for
the junior prom—but blessedly wasn't so hurt she'd never dance
again. When—oh, the list goes on and on for a lifetime, even
when the infirmities of advanced age assaulted her with new
indignities on the hour.

She knew, as all humorists do, that laughter and tears spring
from the same source, sorrow and disappointment. There was a
time for tears, of course, but mostly she believed that crying was

a waste of time because it "didn't accomplish anything." Laughter, on the other hand, was an important defense weapon in her battle to survive. Laughter was her tonic and her psychiatrist—and her gift to me.

Guacamole

Y ou know what I'm craving?" he asked.
   "No, what?"
   "That green gooey stuff they serve with fajitas in Mexican restaurants. What's it called? I can't think of the word—"
   "Hmmm—well, darn, I can't think of it either. If you hadn't asked me I could have rattled it off, but now that you have, it's flown right out of my head. But it's made from avocados."
   "Yes, I know that. I'm not senile, after all. And the best we ever ate was in that little restaurant in San Antonio that time we went to a convention out there—"
   "Yes! The spring of 1991. Best convention we ever went to. Bob and Sue, and Dave and Helen, and that nice couple from Chicago were with us at the restaurant. Helen's cousin who lives in Dallas had recommended it. And we all loved the avocado dip, I remember."
   "Yes, but there's a word for that kind of dip. What is it?"
   "Oh, it'll come to us," she assured him. "But I remember what I wore that night. I had an expensive scarf I'd bought at Delmar's splashed with green and hot pink and blue and black and it hung just so around my shoulders and everyone said it looked great on me. Oh, and those Ferragamo shoes with the grosgrain bows on them."
   "Well, this is driving me crazy. Why can't I think of the word for that green avocado stuff," he said.
   "I wonder whatever happened to that nice couple from Chicago? You know their daughter got dropped from sorority rush at Indiana University and they were absolutely distraught. Thought she might quit school and become a hippie."

"How can you remember the life story of the daughter of some random people from Chicago when you can't pull up the name for that green dip made from avocados? That makes no sense to me. But their name was Hostetter, by the way. He worked in marketing."

"Yes! Sam and Mary Hostetter! Well, I haven't thought of them in years. They were nice. I wonder if they're still alive?"

"Well, if they were, we could call them up and ask them what the word for avocado dip is."

She laughed then. You might as well, she thought. "Oh, it'll come to us. "

"What happened to the daughter? Did she drop out of college?" he asked.

"No, now that I think about it I believe we had a Christmas card one year telling us that she'd graduated from medical school. Sometimes life's disappointments work out for the best."

"I'm pretty sure Sam Hostetter retired a year or two before I did."

"Yes! You're right. Now I remember—they moved back to that small town in Indiana where they'd both grown up. They always wanted us to visit them in Chicago. I wish we had."

"We could still visit them in Indiana," he said.

"New Lisbon! New Lisbon, Indiana, is where they were from."

"Well, let's just drive straight to New Lisbon, Indiana, look up Sam and Mary ask them—"

She interrupted him, "—if they have any GUACAMOLE?"

He laughed then. You might as well.

"Told you it would come to us," she said.

Greetings from Dubai

Greetings From Dubai,

This message might meet you in (utmost surprise), however, it's just my urgent need for foreign partner that made me to contact you for this transaction. I am a banker by profession from United Arab Emirates and currently holding the post of Director Auditing and Accounting unit of the bank.

I have the opportunity of transfering (sic) the left over funds, $17.5 million, our bank deceased customer late Richard Burson, who died on (Egypt Air Flight 990) along with his family on a plane crash below. (http://news.bbc.co.uk/1/hi/.....)

Hence i am inviting you for a business deal where this money can be shared between us in the ratio of 50/50 as a brotherhood.

If you agree to my business proposal further details of the transfer will be forwarded to you as soon as i receive your return mail.

Respectfully
yours
Mr.Kazim Obaid

Dear Mr. Kazim Obaid (may I call you KO?)

First, let me just say right off that your email did indeed come as an (utmost surprise) to me. But having picked myself up off the floor, KO, I hasten to add that it could not have arrived at a more fortuitous moment. You can't imagine how many places I have to put 8.75 million dollars. We need a new roof and a new

83

upstairs furnace at the Lexington house, and the Owen County farm needs a ga-zillion miles of new fence, and the grandchildren all want to go to Disney World, and then Christmas is coming. Well, ha-ha, I guess I don't have to tell you that 8 + million dollars just doesn't go as far as it used to.

Oh, but I'm forgetting myself, KO. Those poor people who died in the plane crash, Mr. Burson and his family! How tragic. And to think they left no will and no heirs. I can only imagine the grief you've endured, and the stress this situation has placed on you. I know it must be very trying to find someone with enough brotherhood in their hearts to take half of this money off your hands. Well KO, you've emailed the right random person in the old US of A. Though I am a sister—not a brother per se—brotherhood bubbles through my veins like the milk of kindness. I am going to help you! Email me back asap and let me know how I can be of service.

Sincerely yours,

Georgia (being as how we're in the brotherhood together now I'm hoping first names are OK with you KO :-))

Dear KO,

I have received your reply, but sadly must inform you that I cannot free up one hundred thousand dollars to deposit in a joint bank account in your name and mine at my local bank. Times are hard here in Kentucky, KO, and the banks, well, they aren't in the mood to lend much money. Yes, yes—I know this will make it impossible for you to transfer Mr. Burson's estate amounting to 17.5 million dollars from a Dubai bank to our joint account at Owenton First and People's. I know that I am losing out on the chance of a lifetime. I am resigned to that. Actually, to tell you the truth, I'm not sure I could fit in with the rich. Thin doesn't come natural to me, and I doubt I could get the hang of playing Polo. But I digress—I still think I can help YOU! Yesterday I received an email out of the blue (talk about Providence! talk about Serendipity!) from a Mr. Benjamin Hark of Nigeria. He is the Senior Accounts Director for Offshore Mortgage and Services for Natwest Bank, London, and he is looking for a partner in a "profitable business investment." Oh, K O, I just have a feeling about Ben Hark! I think he's the answer to your prayers. I am copying his email address on this message to you—you dear, dear man you've been through so much trying to settle this estate. Honestly, you'd think rich people would be more considerate and leave some sort of will, wouldn't you? (Another reason I'd be uneasy hanging out with them—they can be so unthoughtful.)

But I want you to know that I really appreciate all you've tried to do for me, K O, and I wish you and Ben Hark the best of luck and good fortune going forward.

Warmest regards,
From your sister in the brotherhood,
Georgia

P.S. Would you have any interest in purchasing a bridge over Eagle Creek at Natlee, Kentucky? If so, let me know asap by return email. I can get you a deal!

Rhubarb

My book club was planning to read Barbara Kingsolver's new book *Animal, Vegetable, Miracle*—the one about eating locally grown foods exclusively and only those in season—and so the discussion leader turns to me, and says, "And so Georgia, why don't you make Kingsolver's "Month of May" recipe for Rhubarb Crisp on page 89 for our refreshments next month."

I said yes, sure, no problem, I'd love to—even though I've never touched a rhubarb before in my life, even though I'm mostly a counterfeit cook nowadays scooting commercially prepared food into antique dishes and passing it off as home-made. In retrospect, I'm not sure what I was thinking, but I think I was thinking that whipping up a crisp from scratch might move me one degree closer to Barbara Kingsolver, who like me is a Kentucky born writer, except her books make Oprah's Book Club and the short list for the Pulitzer Prize—and I can only wish.

So I set out to find some rhubarb in the asphalt city I now call home. It soon became apparent to me why I've been able to successfully avoid rhubarb for six decades. This vegetable is in the Department of Agriculture's witness protection program. It's spotted from time to time, but it's near impossible to catch up with it.

My first calls went out to several of my friends who are always going on about their abundant, non-pesticide gardens, and like Kingsolver, feed themselves from the land. Each in turn said that they couldn't "get rhubarb to grow!" Hmmm.

Next, I checked the Farmers Market, a delightful traveling carnival of local food producers that encamps on city property here twice a week. Well, to be honest, I didn't check it on Thursday because it was raining cats and dogs and my desire to win a Pulitzer Prize will only push me so far. But it's open on Saturday, too, plenty enough time to pick up some rhubarb for Monday night's to-do, I reasoned.

But on Saturday, I learned it had been a "cold, late spring" in Kentucky. Anywise, the Farmers Market didn't have any rhubarb.

My next stop was the Kroger supermarket closest to my home. I was a little concerned that this was cheating on Kingsolver's philosophy of buying locally grown foods in season. I strongly suspect that the mega-grocer imports its produce from any old locale that has not had a "cold, late spring." But Kroger Inc. is headquartered in Cincinnati, just over the Ohio River from Kentucky, and I decided that gave it a hint of local aura.

"Nope," was the terse response I got when I inquired if they had any rhubarb.

Undaunted, I checked with another Kroger in a trendier neighborhood. They were friendlier and told me they'd been ordering it every week for a month, but had yet to get any. They suggested I try yet another Kroger in an even trendier neighborhood, which I did.

"Had some. Sold it in a hour. Sorry."

By now I was frantic. This was not going to edge me into conversation with the famous Barbara Kingsolver if she should ever drop in to visit her Old Kentucky Home.

And so I started phoning every food market in Lexington. Finally, I located two sources of rhubarb. One was a small organic food boutique on the other side of the city. They refused to verify that their rhubarb had been grown locally, but did verify that it was $3.99 per lb. because, "you know" they said, "it's organic."

The second source—inexplicably—was a big box store a half-mile from my house. No one actually said their rhubarb had been imported from China, but no one said it hadn't been either. It was a $1.99 per lb. Draw your own conclusions.

I faced a moral dilemma: organic and "possibly local," versus cheaper and "possibly Chinese." In the end, my Scottish genes won out, and I rationalized that driving across town to buy organic would leave a larger carbon footprint than running up to the big box store nearby. I bought all Big Box had—twelve stalks—and single-handedly wiped out half the rhubarb supply in Lexington.

In the end, my Rhubarb Crisp was not as crisp as I expected. To be honest, it was downright soggy. So I resorted to my old trick of using pretty dishes to distract guests from the food, and served up my un-crisp on my mother's dessert plates.

Along the way, I learned some interesting facts about rhubarb that may be a conversation opener should Barbara Kingsolver and I ever get a chance to chat. I wonder if she knows, for example, that dramatists as far back as Shakespeare have evoked "a menacing crowd sound" by asking several people to stand close together and repeat the word "rhubarb" over and over. (Personally, I'm thinking all those "menacing" crowds may be what scared rhubarb into hiding.) In time, the word rhubarb was co-opted to describe baseball fans who directed "a menacing crowd sound" at the umpire.

Finally, I learned that rhubarb is indigenous to Mongolia where it grew wild along the Rhubarb Road all the way to ancient Peking. That means that all the rhubarb that has ever been was originally exported from China!

I feel less guilty now about having bought my rhubarb at the Big Box.

Coffee and Lard

Well, as Will Rogers said, "All I know is what I read in the papers." On Monday, a report came out saying that coffee—even lots of coffee—is good for your heart. Another study claims it lowers the risk of type II diabetes, and yet another that it helps prevent colon and prostate cancer. It boosts mood and stops headaches. It cuts the risk of developing both Parkinson's disease and tooth cavities, and even slashes cirrhosis of the liver. They've now concluded that drinking coffee extends one's lifespan. Coffee is the new health food, ready to challenge broccoli and whole-wheat toast.

I've been a three cups a day gal for most of my life, sinfully slurping away, as one expert after another warned me it was bad for my health. Now my guilt has been washed down the drain with the coffee grounds, and overnight I've been transformed into a health food consumer.

I wish my parents could have lived to see coffee elevated to the status of a miracle drug. Daddy, especially, with his broad sense of humor, would have gotten a kick out of it. He and Mother both loved coffee, and the coffeepot was always hot in their kitchen. Before guests could sputter hello, he would order them to "sit down and have a cup of coffee." Now he would be adding, "Doctor's orders!"

Of course, Mother intuitively knew coffee was good for her. It was her Geritol, her energizing elixir. Pushing through a long life of arthritis pain and other nagging illnesses, she'd say every morning, "Let me have one more cup to get going." And sure enough, coffee rarely failed her.

It's not surprising then that I married a man who is also obsessed with coffee. Ernie fell into the habit of drinking it at all

89

hours to get through twelve-hour days at the office. Then one Christmas, someone gave him an electric grinder, and the rest, as they say, is history. He turned into a coffee connoisseur grinding up the likes of "Big Blue Blend" fresh every morning. He sniffs coffee beans like others do wine corks. Given the amount of coffee he drinks, I predict he will live to be 101 like Uncle Bo, who, by the way, enjoyed a hot cup or two every morning.

I was still reeling from the news of coffee's sprint to the top of the food pyramid when I ran across an article touting lard as the new organic fat. That would be lard, the greasy, gooey stuff we used to render on the farm at hog killing time. Hogs were always butchered in the dead of winter so the meat wouldn't spoil before it could be consumed or cured. It's not a pretty scene, slopping around in January muck with a frantic pig, and I've spent a lifetime trying to repress images of hog killings. I enjoy a ham sandwich a lot more if I don't think too much about it.

But back to lard, the chic new organic item on the menu. We rendered the melted fat of the pig into silver looking five-gallon tin containers that we wittily called—lard cans. Lard cans were our object d' art, useful folk creations worthy of cradling an organic health food. We turned empty ones into flowerpots for the front porch, and if chairs were scarce we sat on them like stools. You could also store pictures and newspaper clippings in them.

Before it was empty, though, we'd dip out of a lard can for weeks or even months with a large, bent tablespoon much the same way the young clerks at Baskin-Robbins reach down into huge pails of ice cream. Lard is pretty in large quantities. It looks like gallons and gallons of white, fluffy cake icing.

Ignorance was bliss in that innocent time before we knew about cholesterol, and we emptied a lot of lard cans. Later on, when lard was accused of murdering half the local population, we stuck up for it. The best cooks that ever were—people like my mother and my aunts—said lard could not be equaled for making a flakey piecrust or biscuit dough or for frying chicken. Lard was missed when it was forced into exile.

They'd be pleased to know that lard has now been rehabilitated and is respectable again. But having seen more than a few hog killings, they'd be put-off, I suspect, by the stuck-up airs

90

lard is putting on in organic food markets. In fact, I wonder if people would be so enchanted with the notion of organic-anything if they'd spent time on a farm. Organic often seems to me to be a code word for things we can't talk about in polite society, like fertilizer that starts out as cow manure.

But who am I to argue with the newspapers? I'm sending Ernie out now to a natural foods store to locate some "Peruvian Organic Blend" coffee beans that have been roasted in lard.

Becky the Albino

Maybe you won't appreciate this little story if you've never felt different, if you've never been a teenager or can't remember being one.

And maybe you can't laugh at this silliness if you've walked a road so divergent it rises up to taunt you every morning of your life. I think of those who've struggled with racial prejudice or serious physical or mental disabilities.

But my daughter Becky laughed when she told this to me, and so did I. We laughed until—well, I'm getting ahead of the story.

I neither boast nor apologize for the genetic heritage I passed on to my children. I admit that had I had a say in the matter, I would have nixed our family's flat feet and ratcheted up our athletic ability. But our three daughters are healthy and funny and kind, and thanks to their father's side of the family, they can sing like songbirds.

But we do not tan. We are, as one plain-spoken black child pointed out to us in the park one day, "the whitest white people" he'd ever seen.

Pigment bleached out of my DNA before I was a gleam in my father's eye. Daddy was a tow-headed blonde, and Mother a true redhead with colorless eyebrows and eyelashes.

They came of age before movie stars in the 1950s made the sun-tanned look *de rigueur*. And so they couldn't understand why I fretted about being pale as a ghost. They were prone to going on and on about how popular my looks would have been in the 18th century—or maybe it was the Middle Ages— whenever my pasty coloring was in vogue. I never understood why they thought that line of reasoning would comfort me, but after a few third degree sunburns, I gave up on getting a tan.

What others don't understand is that my daughters and I don't tan. Not with any kind of lotion. Not in a tanning bed. Not even in the Caribbean. Our sunburned skin peels off like a snake's, and underneath we're as pale as ever.

Two of my daughters accepted their genetic fate philosophically, and with auburn and blonde hair, respectively, our sun-crazed culture cuts their paleness a little slack. Our middle daughter Becky, however, inherited her father's dark hair and eyes but my ivory skin. She's Snow White come to life, and in my opinion, she's beautiful. But Becky railed against what she called her "cartoon looks" convinced that tanned skin was the key to success—and happiness—in life.

Perhaps she had a point if one were wading through high school, like Becky, in the late 1980s and early 90s in Flatwoods, Kentucky. That was the exact place and precise moment in history when tanning beds and Farrah Fawcett's big hair collided.

Becky mastered Farrah's pumpkin sized hair, but the baked orange skin her friends cooked up at the tanning salon was beyond her grasp. High school wits, usually boys, taunted her everyday. "Hey, Dracula, don't you ever go outside?" "Oh my gosh, it's the Abominable Snowman!"

I found myself in my parents' place, rambling on about the 18th century and the Middle Ages, urging her to accept herself, and reminding her that confidence is a large part of attractiveness. Need I add that my advice fell on deaf ears?

The summer before her senior year in high school, however, Becky snagged a job at an upscale boutique at the new mall in downtown Ashland. She discovered she had a knack for putting together stylish ensembles not only for herself but for others. This flair, combined with her outgoing personality, made her a hit with customers. Her boss was delighted with her, and I was pleased to see Becky's confidence growing every week. It was no surprise to me when her newfound self-esteem began to attract the positive attention she'd wanted from young men.

One day during her lunch break, she walked to the opposite end of the mall to pick up an item at Walmart. She was full of herself, striding along the aisles at the discount store in her expensive crocheted vest and black bell bottom slacks, knowing she looked fantastic, wondering who might be looking at her, admiring her—

Her Walter Mitty daydream imploded when she nearly collided with two elderly men approaching her in the aisle. Always polite, Becky took particular pains to show respect to them as she apologized for her inattention. With their unkempt clothing and disheveled hair, she thought they might be homeless.

Then, as they moved on, Becky overheard one man say to the other in a flat, nasal, local accent, "I think that's one of them there albinos."

That night, telling me the story, Becky laughed at herself. That night I think Becky stopped seeing herself only in the reflection of other people's eyes.

Georgeann
and the End of the World

If Christians were raptured up to Heaven last Saturday as that fellow in California predicted, I didn't know anybody good enough to make the cut. Since I hang out with a lot of churchgoing folk most every Sunday, that's a disconcerting thought.

All this talk last weekend about the world ending, though, set me to thinking about my stint as our church's youth leader. Now before anybody accuses me of heresy and suggests I be hanged by the World Council of Churches, let me say right up front that all I'm trying to do here is tell a story. It's a true one, a little sad and a little funny, but I'm not in the business of making theological statements. I leave that to those more qualified.

In the United Methodist Church, however, even the unqualified, like me, are often pressed to work above our pay grade. And so I zoomed to the top echelon of leadership in the UM Youth Fellowship the same way I became a Girl Scout leader—by showing up at a meeting that everybody else skipped.

Our oldest daughter, Shan, thirteen and a freshman in high school, was excited about being old enough to join the senior UMYF group at our little church. Poof—just like that there was no leader to help guide this handful of teenagers through adolescence. We couldn't afford a youth minister, the senior pastor was over-worked as it was, and when her last child left for college, the former parent-leader begged to retire after ten years of service. Actually she went on a hunger strike to emphasize her point, but that's a tale for another day.

There seemed nothing for me to do but say yes and blunder forward. As my minister gently pointed out, I had once taught in

95

high school so how hard could it be? Well, sleeping on the floor at the youth group lock-ins proved to be pretty hard in my opinion.

And my administration ran into other problems, too. Because of my husband's business travel, meeting-time often found me without childcare for my two younger girls. I fell into the habit of taking Becky, age 11, and Georgeann, age 9, along with me, with vague instructions to "be good." To Shan's distress, they were soon participating members of the group.

I also used up my program ideas more quickly than I had thought possible. Then I remembered the football coach in the old Funky Winkerbean comic strip who showed a film every day of his teaching career. That's when I hit upon the idea of renting a series of 16 mm movies—this was before the easy era of DVDS—about the end of the world.

I sincerely thought these films would be interesting for the group to discuss. But I was also struck that it was a four part series, and would fill up a month of meetings.

And so we plunged into our study of the Book of Revelations, the blind leading the blind. What I hadn't reckoned on was the Hollywood influence on the filmmakers. Have you ever seen "The Creature from the Black Lagoon" or other B-grade science-fiction horror movies popular in the 1950s and 60s? Despite my misgivings about the quality of the films, the UMYF kids loved them!

The movies began with decadent scenes of modern life, and then progressed to the Rapture of the few good people on earth. Oddly, most folks were making a cake when whisked off to Heaven. Many of the main characters, of course, were left behind to puzzle over electric mixers gone wild and the sudden plethora of unbaked cake batter.

The Tribulation of the earth came next—and I'm pretty sure it lasted longer than the five months Mr. Camping projects. At least it extended through three of our movie installments.

Each week our meetings ended with frightened teenagers crying and asking questions I had difficulty answering. Some of the hardest ones came from my nine-year-old daughter, Georgeann, a serious child who would grow up to be a clinical psychologist.

One late afternoon during that fall, I was busy cooking supper when I looked at the clock and realized I should have picked up Shan from band practice ten minutes earlier. Becky and Georgeann were playing in their friends' yard down the street as they often did after school, and wouldn't come home until I called them for supper—even then under protest since they'd rather play than eat.

Knowing that the high school was nearby and that I could go and return home in less than ten minutes, I dashed off without rounding them up. I'd be back before they knew I'd been gone, I reasoned. I'd never done that before, but it was a pretty day, Shan was stranded in the school parking lot, and I made a not-perfect-mom split second decision.

Unbeknown to me, however, Georgeann hadn't gone with Becky to play at the neighbor's. Instead, she'd vanished to the basement rec-room where she was quietly cutting out magazine pictures for an on-going scrapbook of her life as she hoped it would someday be. (Have I mentioned that Georgeann was a deep child?)

So of course she emerged from the basement about three minutes after I drove out of the driveway. A casserole was bubbling in the oven. Salad fixings were scattered on the cutting board. But I was not there. And neither of her sisters was there. For the first time in her life, she found herself alone in the house. She reached the only logical conclusion.

When I returned home a few minutes later, she was near hysteria. Finally, to snap her out of it, I said the only thing I thought might get through to a nine-year-old brain.

"Georgeann, do you really think God would rapture Becky up to Heaven and leave you behind?"

She thought about that a minute and then, between sobs, laughed.

"No, she's badder than me."

So maybe the world did end last Saturday, and I'm too arrogant to believe I'm one of Georgeann's badder ones who got left behind.

Mr. Bear

Last week, I tagged along with my youngest daughter, Georgeann, to the Kentucky side of Cincinnati. Her young children, Annelise and Hudson, made the jaunt from Lexington with us. At five and almost three, they are now almost exactly the ages my two older daughters were when Georgeann was born. Strapped in the backseat in their state-of-the-art car carriers, with a movie playing on the DVD player and iPads loaded with games clutched in their hands, the children didn't make a peep on the seventy-mile trip. Quite a contrast, I thought, to the long car trips of my young motherhood when I had only my imagination to keep the children entertained and separated in their minimally restrained seats.

But the moment we hit the six-lane traffic of I-75—a stretch of city driving that puts me on edge—Annelise began to screech in a voice edged with panic. "Mr. Bear! Mr. Bear! Mr. Bear! Hudson is grabbing Mr. Bear!"

I turned around to investigate, and sure enough, there was Hudson with a big old grin on his face pulling as hard as he could on Mr. Bear's head while Annelise held on to his body for dear life. Like a member of the family, Mr. Bear has been her near constant companion since she was an infant. Hudson is never allowed to touch Mr. Bear unless Annelise gives him permission for the occasional cuddle. (This is in no way a deprivation since their household has a few hundred stuffed animals lying around. Okay, that's an exaggeration but not a large one.)

Déjà vu. Staring at my grandchildren pulling at opposite ends of Mr. Bear's fragile body, I was transported back to 1977 on this same stretch of Interstate highway. Mother was with me then, sitting in the front passenger seat where I was now, and an infant Georgeann was cradled in her arms in those pre-safety-seat days. I was at the wheel navigating unfamiliar urban traffic to pick up my husband at the Greater Cincinnati Airport.

My five-year-old daughter Shan was in the back seat with Bear whom she never left at home. A plump half-pillow, half-plaything, he was handmade from a cloth cut-out, a craft notion popular in that era. The girls' other grandmother had found Bear's blue front and back body images at a fabric store, sewed his exterior edges together, and in the process, stuffed him full of foam pieces. The result was a rotund pillow-bear.

My mother-in-law had made a similar stuffed animal for our middle daughter Becky when she came along, but Becky could not be persuaded that her brown Dog was as fine as Shan's blue Bear. And so, as I-75 widened from two lanes into many lanes, and the lightening fast traffic converged and diverged from all directions, Becky, a few months shy of her third birthday, grabbed Shan's Bear by the head.

A frantic tug of war broke out, punctuated with shrieks and sobs. Mother, holding the baby in the front seat, could do little to intervene in the battle. I, of course, couldn't cross multiple lanes of traffic to pull onto a shoulder if our lives had depended on it. My admonitions to "JUST STOP IT!" were ignored. (Where was Dr. Spock when you needed him?)

Tension was escalating in both the front and back seats of our car when suddenly the girls, in unison, let out a blood-curdling scream. I nearly lunged into an eight wheeler in an adjacent lane. What had happened? Had one of the back doors swung open despite being locked? Had someone fallen out of the car into the path of the semi-trucks?

Bear's decapitation is what had happened. His head was in Becky's hands, his body in Shan's, and his foam innards were flying all over the car like popcorn on steroids. Bear had lost his mind—and I was not far behind him.

Then, as both girls sobbed inconsolably in the back seat, Mother began to laugh and laugh until tears ran down her face. "You might as well," she said.

Mother's laughter restored both Bear and me to sanity. Within a few days, we had him re-stuffed and his head reat-

99

tached with heavy thread. He soldiered on for many more years until his skin completely gave way to ravels and gaping holes. Then, we let him go to that special place in our hearts where we forever hold all of those we have loved.

Last week, my hand darted into the backseat in time to rescue Annelise's Mr. Bear before his body gave way. But I heard my mother's voice echo across the decades to remind both Georgeann and me that you have to keep a sense of humor when dealing with the day-to-day challenges of parenting young children. You might as well laugh, she would say. I would add that it sure beats losing either your head or your mind.

Night People
versus
Morning People

The world is divided into two kinds of people, those who rise with the sun and those who don't. The morning folks cornered the world market on worms centuries ago, and have the best PR staff in the business. Early to rise, makes a man healthy, wealthy and wise—well, their press releases go on and on.

Personally, I don't think I've ever seen the sun come up. Oh, maybe in my youth when I pulled colicky babies through the night, but I lived in Ashland then, in a hilly forest cut off from the rest of the natural world by industrial smog. Like the monuments at Stonehenge, smokestacks circled my house in the woods. It would be night, and then morning, but the light arrived in the sky without a splash of poetry.

I've also driven family members to the hospital at the crack of dawn for early a.m. surgeries, but in my memory it was always sleeting. The sun got out of bed reluctantly, like me, on those mornings, incognito in a raincoat and galoshes.

I confess that I enjoy sleeping through the sun's salutation, and when I rise, I touch the new day gently, like fragile stemware that will shatter if I grasp it with too much enthusiasm. I do not speak to others. I wiggle my toes to make sure I'm still alive. I look at my husband to make sure he is still alive. (Our mutual aversion to sunrises may have contributed to the longevity of our marriage.) I stagger to the kitchen like Dolly Parton to pour myself a cup of ambition. One cup. Two cups. Sometimes three.

101

You cannot have too much caffeine in the morning in my opinion. I read the newspaper in silence, word for word, from the back section to the front, and update my worry list about the world. With that arduous task behind me, I drink a Diet Pepsi. I repeat—you cannot consume too much caffeine in the morning in my opinion. Then, maybe, I shower and dress. On a really good day, though, now that I'm old and retired, I sit down at the computer to think and write, and don't dress until lunchtime.

The problem with being a slow starter is that the morning people think you are more decadent than you are. When they pop by at noon and find you in your bathrobe, they jump to the conclusion that you've succumbed to drugs or alcohol, and stage an intervention.

My mother, bless her, was a morning person. Late in her life, she was fond of calling me at 8 a.m. to recite the long list of chores she'd accomplished that day—getting around on a walker, mind you. Then she would ask in a maleficent voice that managed to sound cheery and innocent, "What have you done today?"

We late-starters get no points for polishing the silver at 11 p.m. or writing a novel at midnight. Never mind that our list of life accomplishments equals that of most others, that we manage to raise children, put food on the table and cash in the bank. We don't get it done soon after daybreak—so it isn't quite virtuous.

Sigh. It's our dang DNA, scientists now say. A lack of pep and gusto in the early morning, researchers have concluded, is wired into our biological hard drive. Even my mother conceded that I cried most of the night when she brought me home from the hospital, and then slept much of my first day at home. I have no memories, either, of being one of those annoying toddlers who get up before the rest of the household to dump boxes of cereal onto the middle of the kitchen floor. No, they always had to shake me awake when it was time to get going on another day.

I'm left now with a haunting image of my primeval ancestor staying up late into the night to skin and prep the game some early bird dragged back to the cave at sunrise and dumped on her bearskin bed. I'm sure she got no credit, no none at all, for her contributions to the tribe's survival.

Unless—could it be—she discovered that wishes made on the "first star I see tonight" come true?

Could she have been the first person to see the cow jump over the moon, or to sing "Twinkle, twinkle little star ... " and shush the babes to sleep?

Could it be that our circadian rhythm does not define our character?

Could it be that Ben Franklin wasn't as smart as he thought he was?

Casual Dress

The late comedian, George Goebel, described himself as the guy in the brown suit at a black tie event. "How do they know?" he would wonder with a plaintive tone in his voice.

Today old George would be more perplexed than ever at what to wear. Leastwise, I am, and I suspect I'm not alone. Remember the flap over the flip-flops those college girls wore when they received an award from President Bush in the Rose Garden? The media ridiculed their bare feet and splashed photographs of their pedicures all across America. I felt sorry for them. Coming of age when "business attire" and "church clothes" have vanished from the language, how could they know that rubber beach thongs are not dressy enough for a White House ceremony?

Personally, I have no clue what to wear either unless I'm the mother of the bride or I'm going to bed. All other occasions fall into the vast wasteland known as "casual dress" or the baffling black hole called "dressy casual." From wrinkled shorts slept in overnight to *haute couture*, you roll the dice and take your chances.

I blame this confusion, like everything else wrong in our society, on America's bankers. Back in the old days before they started wearing blue jeans and tee shirts to work on Casual Fridays, I usually could figure out what was appropriate to wear in social situations. I never thought it was a good idea for bankers to get too comfortable when handling our money, and the current financial crisis has proved me right.

Now no one agrees on what "casual dress" or—shudder—"dressy casual" means on an invitation. The best I can figure out, these phrases mean different things depending on what part of the country you're in. For example, one of our daughters went to school in Boston, and I soon realized that if you wore any color other than gray or brown up there, or any jewelry whatsoever, you were over-dressed. The apparent objective was to blend into the winter landscape—a season that stretched from September to June. If an occasion were "dressy casual," however, it was permissible to wear a pair of small earrings—silver with your gray sweater, gold with your brown one. Before I caught on, I once wore a red shirt and matching hoop earrings out to eat in a restaurant and nearly ruined our daughter socially.

Another daughter, though, went to school in South Carolina where it's always the Fourth of July. Bright, colorful sundresses, shorts, and cute, floral Capri pants were *de rigueur*. Let me just say now that South Carolina casual is not flattering on a woman who can remember when Dwight D. Eisenhower was president. I nearly ruined that daughter socially, too.

And then there's Texas. Down there they wear all the jewelry they own with their bathing suits and do their hair to go to bed. I'm thinking maybe Texas sets the standard for "dressy casual." At least, it's no surprise to me that Texas has had more Miss Americas than any other state. Those women flat out try harder.

People under thirty, though, wherever they're from, tend to think "dressy casual" means a clean pair of jeans and maybe a pressed shirt. The first time we took our son-in-law to the races at Keeneland Clubhouse, he went into shock when he realized he was not going to be admitted wearing jeans, even if he put on a borrowed jacket and tie. He apparently thought we were pulling his leg (metaphorically speaking) when we told him denim was not permitted.

I will give him this—here in Kentucky the nuances of casual are hard to nail down even for men. Kentucky guy casual runs the gamut from a UK sweatshirt to a GQ sweater slung across the shoulder, from dirty sneakers to Gucci loafers. The women are harder to peg. I can never guess which direction casual will tilt. If I show up in my black blazer, everybody else will be wearing sweatsuits—or sequined sweaters and velvet pants!

Now I've been invited to an event at a fancy hotel in Florida. The invitation suggested "resort casual dress." I don't know if that is sub-prime casual as in code for "bathing suits just dandy" or high "dressy casual" as in "bring on the rhinestone bling." So I've decided to wear my flip-flops and black blazer. I figure a woman who remembers the Eisenhower administration is probably invisible at a resort no matter what she has on.

Narcissistic Me

I read a fascinating study (I love that word, study) in yester-day's Lexington *Herald-Leader*. It quoted people with impressive titles at the University of Kentucky and at other institutions, but boiled down the article simply said that a lot of narcissistic people are drawn to Facebook.

Narcissistic, in case you have not been paying attention, is every talking head's favorite new word. It has replaced "self-esteem"—which was a good thing promoted by talk show hosts, self-help books, and nurtured by teachers and parents *en masse*. When you've lived as long as I have, though, you know that all good things have to end up in a bad place eventually.

Apparently, that bad place is Facebook, a cesspool of narcissism. Up to now, I've been celebrating my discovery of "social media." I've considered it the 21st century version of Nick's Grocery Store where people around Natlee and New Columbus gathered when I was a kid to catch up on what was happening in everybody's else's lives.

Yes—a tiny bit of embellishment and maybe even some bragging filled the hours folks spent on those hard benches that lined one side of the store. But there was also a lot of laughter at the absurdities of our world. There was shared grief when a friend experienced loss or was in trouble. Political disagreements filled many an hour at Nick's, and celebration was genuine when one among us achieved something worth, well, celebrating. Anyone's achievement in that small place was owned by everyone.

In fact, I've ever been amazed at the absence of jealousy in the world of my childhood. Achievement by any of "ours" was "our" achievement too, and touted and repeated to others. The same was true of trouble. If any who lived in the boundaries of our world—or if their parents or siblings or grandparents did—then their illness, their tragedy, their loss, was claimed as our own.

And so I innocently wandered into the Facebook community and was delighted to find myself to home. Now, after reading this study, I realize that I may not be a good neighbor after all, but a narcissist, which I infer is a notch below being a Communist. I searched the article in vain for evidence that I was NOT a narcissist.

First, a narcissist posts "sexy" pictures of herself on her Facebook wall. Well, at my age, I have little sexy left, but I do confess to using a three-year-old "thin" profile picture taken at my daughter's wedding. For months, I'd eaten nothing but foamy diet milkshakes to get that thin, to get into that expensive suit. Since it's likely I will never be that thin again unless I'm stricken by a fatal illness, I enjoy memorializing that image. Also, when I put up photo albums on Facebook of the family, our daughters and sons-in-law and the grands, I confess to posting only "the good ones." Is everyone else posting their "bad ones?"

I don't, however, fall into the narcissist's category regarding the language I use. I don't use profanity on Facebook. Maybe, though, I can't get credit for not doing that because I don't use profanity anywhere. Profanity doesn't come naturally to me. I blame Mother for that. She didn't allow it in her house or her world. She in turn was raised by a mother who would not allow her to use the word "bull" to describe the male of the bovine species that pastured on our farm. They were to always be called "males."

According to the study, a narcissist also can be spotted on Facebook by her use of third person rather than first person pronouns when referring to herself. I got real excited about that revelation because I use I all the time! But then I got to thinking about the big words I toss in, a reflection of the old English teacher nerdy me, and decided I couldn't get credit for that either.

I also enjoy "admiration and recognition." Sigh. When somebody "likes" a column, blog entry or funny I've posted, I admit I "like" it. But I also "like" lots of other people's posts about their trips, pictures, grandchildren's achievements, family gatherings, photos of flowers, comings and goings and doings. I genuinely "like" knowing about the lives of my friends.

All this to justify telling you in my narcissistic way—I lost two more pounds at my Weight Watchers weigh-in yesterday. Please "admire and recognize" me enough to get me through another week from the word my Mother's voice won't let me type.

The Hudson Brothers: l-r, Georgia's G-uncle Bert, her grandfather George, G-uncle Dick, G-uncle Murphy. Seated, l-r, Georgia's grandmother Monnie Hudson, G-aunt Elizabeth, and G-aunt Bessie. Fall 1940.

Demi Moore Stew

The word was stew. I pitched Ernie the perfect clue: Dinty Moore. Sigh. He thought I said Demi Moore and shouted back, "Naked!"

Then there was the time my daughter Georgeann and I were partners. False teeth was the answer I needed to pull from her, so I said, "something old people have."

"Cadillacs!" she said without missing a beat.

But my mother was the most unpredictable partner I ever played Taboo with. I fed her the best synonym for "matrimony" that I could think of, "marriage."

She replied with confidence. "Man!"

"Well," she said when I took her to task for blowing such an obvious clue, "that's what marriage means to me. A man."

I'm not sure how Mother would have fared in the gender PC world of today.

So yes, we enjoy playing board games in our family, the ones like Taboo and Password and Apples to Apples that revolve around words. Partly, that's because I'm not good with numbers and don't do so well at cards and the like. But the word games make us laugh a lot and remind us that what is obvious to one person is not necessarily obvious to another, even those we love and live with.

The Class Reunion

The class reunion is Life's Great Leveler. Well, maybe not at the ten-year mark—I'll admit that one's cutthroat. But after the first couple of decades, it's a mutual celebration of survival. The very important person is one of the gang again. The man whose life has been filled with disappointments is still quick witted and fun. The shy are emboldened to speak to the popular, who are so relieved to know that somebody still likes them that they confess they always felt shy in high school too. Nobody has escaped pain in some form or another. Compassion, not competition, is the order of the day.

And class reunions can be funny. One of my favorite stories came from my friend Richard after he attended a big number year (no need to be more specific) get-together for his Owen County High School graduating class. As soon as he arrived at the party, a pretty woman came running up to him, threw her arms around him, and hugged him tightly. While he was still reeling from her enthusiasm, she confessed, "I know I still love you—but who are you?"

His old girlfriend, he later learned, had suffered a minor stroke that had impaired her memory, though not her affection.

Another friend (I'll call her Innocent) has given me permission to share this story as long as all names are changed to protect the guilty (whom I'll call Confused.) During our freshman year at Transylvania University, Innocent had one, single date with Confused. There was no spark between them, and after a pleasant evening at the movies and a handshake at the front door of the women's dorm, they returned to their "just friends" status.

At our 25th Class Reunion, however, Confused reminded Innocent of that date and alluded to the sizzling chemistry that had existed between them. She said his memory was inconsistent with hers, but he was not dissuaded. She let it drop for the sake of the evening's civility.

But at the 30th reunion, Confused brought up their hot date again, and expanded it into multiple dates. Innocent was flabbergasted. The more she protested, however, the more adamant he became that they had once been an item. When she insisted her memory failed her, and pressed him for details, he mentioned specific events such as fraternity formal dances they'd attended together and when.

At the 35th gathering, Innocent was ready for him. "Listen here," she said. "Even allowing for drunken amnesia on my part, the time frame you give for our so-called romance was the same year I was pinned to the president of your fraternity. Do you honestly think that you would have been squiring me to fraternity functions right under his nose?"

Without a moment's hesitation, Confused dropped his eyes, and said, "No, you're right, it wasn't you." Then, he went on in a wistful tone.

"But it could have been."

"It could have been" is a pretty good theme for any class reunion, I suppose. But I think I'll vote for "I know I still love you."

Whoever you are.

Expiration Dates

The other day, I was throwing together a hash brown potato casserole at the last minute for a potluck family reunion when I realized the recipe called for a can of Campbell's Cream of Mushroom soup, an item I'd forgotten to pick up on my run to the grocery store. But not to worry, I thought. Over a lifetime, Cream of Mushroom has provided my own small glimpse into the miracle of the loaves and the fishes. Every time I reach into the kitchen pantry there's one more red and white can, somewhere, back in the back, behind the kidney beans, hanging out with the canned tomatoes.

And it was no different this time. At the moment I'd almost given up, my fingers clutched a Cream of Mushroom in the very back corner of the shelf. It was lying behind a jar of artichokes I bought on a whim two years ago when I thought I might whip up hot artichoke dip for the family on Christmas Eve but then I ran out of time and didn't.

I don't know what made me check the "Use By" date that the Campbell folks had stamped on the bottom of the soup can. Usually I don't bother because I can't decipher the itsy numbers without my reading glasses, and they're always cavorting somewhere else without me. But on that day the stars aligned. My glasses were behaving appropriately in place, and before I knew what I was doing, I was reading Cream of Mushroom's obituary. It had expired a week earlier. How could I not have known? Why didn't the artichokes call 911?

"Do you think there is life after death for Cream of Mushroom soup?" I asked my husband. He stopped shoving Diet Pepsi cans and bottles of tea into the iced cooler we were taking to the picnic, and said carefully, "Why do you ask?" He and I are both on high alert for the first signs of dementia in the other.

"Well, what I'm asking is whether it would be safe to toss an expired can of Cream of Mushroom into the hash brown potato casserole because we don't have time to run to the store for another can, and this one died a week ago."

He looked relieved that I was still in the land of the sane. "Why don't you open it up and do an autopsy?" he suggested.

And so I did that. I dumped its rotund body out on a clean white plate and examined it under the harsh overhead lights of my kitchen. To be honest, if I hadn't known better, I wouldn't have known that soup was dead. It looked as lively as Cream of Mushroom can ever manage to look which is to say not very. As gray and ashen as it was on the day of its birth, its jellied innards puddled ever so slightly under my glare.

But botulism bacteria, I've heard, are invisible to the naked eye, and so are salmonella's and all sorts of other nasty microorganisms that could send the potluck crowd en masse to the hospital emergency room. What to do, what to do?

I've faced these dilemmas before. For example, if the milk expires at midnight on August 18 is it okay to use it on the grandchildren's breakfast cereal on August 19? Even if I, myself, am willing to walk on the wild side, what might milk that's eight hours dead do to a delicate two-year-old's digestive tract?

I've often wondered, too, about the psychological impact these expiration dates have on the food itself. Do the eggs go a little crazy knowing the exact day they're going to reach their "Use By" deadline? Do they weep uncontrollably or party hardy on the Thursday night before the Friday execution pre-destined from their conception? And cereal, breakfast's dull companion—is it too dim-witted to understand that its days are numbered? Or does a sense of mortality add depth and meaning to its tedious days?

In the end, Ernie and I were unwilling to risk the well being of the potluck crowd. We decided to toss the expired Cream of Mushroom into the garbage disposal, and dash through the KFC drive-through en route to the party for some expensive fried chicken instead.

But with my own expiration date drawing ever nearer, I was intrigued by an article I ran across on the Internet a few days later. An organization called ShelfLifeAdvice.com has released a study conducted by all sorts of experts who determined that if stored properly, most foods, even eggs and milk, are safe to consume for days after the 'use by' date. Peanut butter can be good for months longer than expected, cereal is safe for a year past its prime, and multiple years can be added to the life expectancy of dry goods like flour and rice, and yes, even to canned goods like Cream of Mushroom.

Maybe then it's possible that I, too, can extend my own shelf life with proper care. Whatever the outcome, though, I don't want to end up sour like the milk or scrambled like the eggs.

In my reckless youth, I often ignored canned biscuits in the back of the fridge until they exploded like firecrackers on the Fourth of July. Would that we could all leave here like the Pillsbury Doughboy, way past our "best if used by" date—and with a glorious hurrah.

Funeral Fun

It occurred to me the other day that I've reached an age in life when I go to more funerals than I do baby showers. Even so, I haven't equaled the record of the Kentucky man I read about who hasn't missed a local funeral in over twenty years. A self-appointed professional mourner, he even attends services for people he doesn't know. It's an odd sort of perfect attendance record, I'll admit, but I've heard of stranger life goals, and it must be reassuring for the folks in his hometown to know that at least one person in these busy times will show up to bid them adieu.

I'm not sure he cries though. That would be left to an eastern Kentucky woman a friend told me about who weeps on behalf of the common weal. She shows up, uninvited, in public places to weep silently whenever tears are needed. That struck me as a mighty fine civic service, and I think each community should have a designated weeper, a sort of common man's poet laureate to keep us in touch with our inner selves.

My Aunt Bessie and Uncle Murphy Hudson, however, were neither town-eccentrics nor town criers, but they did enjoy a good funeral. If the deceased were not too closely kin to them, they viewed a funeral as a convivial place to catch up with old friends. They could usually be counted on to fill a pew and to linger afterwards for mingling and conversation.

They had a point. If grief doesn't get in the way, if one's personal life is not devastated by the departure of the dearly—an old fashioned Kentucky funeral can make for a pretty nice reunion. It's not exactly an exuberant Irish Wake, mind you, but a pleasant get-together nevertheless. Distant cousins and old classmates scatter across summer lawns, laughing softly and

116

catching up on the happenings of the years. Neighbors crowd into the corners of winter rooms and whisper about the achievements of their children and the price of cattle.

But these spontaneous reunions can be a problem for friends and family members from out of town. They always lose at the Do-You-Know-Who-I-Am Game. My friend Professor Jack Higgs insists that the state legislature should pass a law making nametags mandatory for all funeral guests. These would be along the order of "Hi, I'm so and so," and the undertaker would be legally required to stand at the front door with a magic marker, and hand out the peel and seal badges as people enter.

After a family funeral where his elderly aunt asked over and over in her loudest voice, "WHO'S DEAD?" he suggests that maybe it would be a good idea for the corpse to wear ID too. It might read, "Hello. My name is Jack. Thank you for coming."

Oh, everybody seems to have had an experience as surreal as Jack's. As he says, when life gets this absurd, this awful, laughing is about all that can get you through.

For example, our former neighbor was late to her own funeral. Cora passed away in a distant state, but per her instructions, she was flown back to Kentucky to be buried beside her husband. The time of the service at the mausoleum had been published in the paper, the minister had been engaged, and a carefully planned catered lunch had been arranged at a local restaurant for family and close friends. Cora, however, missed her connector flight and showed up a day too late. Thank goodness, she'd requested a closed casket service, so the party was able to go on without her.

Aunt Bessie and Uncle Murphy's only child, James Hudson, grew up to become an undertaker, perhaps, he says, because he attended so many funerals with them when he was a kid. James told this story, and swears it's true, about a woman who died at a very advanced age. Her only remaining relative was an elderly daughter who specified that there be no funeral or graveside rites. The daughter wanted an unembellished interment for her mother, and she, herself, would watch the burial from a limousine parked a few thousand yards away on the street that ran in front of the cemetery.

Standing at the open grave, however, my cousin and his assistant found themselves feeling uncomfortable with this total lack of ceremony. After a few minutes of awkward silence, the assistant said that maybe they should say a little something, at least, maybe a non-denominational prayer? And my cousin James, becoming ever more irritated at the woman watching them silently from the far curb, said yes, do that. It seemed wrong, he went on, to lower someone into the ground who had lived for nearly one hundred years without some small acknowledgment. So the assistant opened his mouth, and out came the only prayer he could remember:

I pledge allegiance to the flag . . .

Classic Flu

Well, I came down with the flu, and I haven't been the same since. Actually, my doctor called it Classic Flu, which as far as I can tell, has nothing at all in common with Classic Coke or classic cars. I've had Classic Flu at least once before, but in my extreme youth. Back then, I nonchalantly drank Classic Coke as though it were nothing special, and my family drove a classic car, too, except we called it our new Chevy. So I guess it's no surprise that I didn't immediately recognize this old bug as a classic when it sidled up to me and whispered, "Don't I know you from someplace?"

Day One: After exchanging small talk for about half a day, Classic Flu was itching for a debate. I had other plans, however, and didn't want to waste my Saturday with any lowlife virus (I didn't yet know I was dealing with a classic, remember.) I gargled, took some Tylenol, and said, "Shoo, fly, shoo." My lack of respect apparently infuriated Classic Flu, and without further discussion, it flexed its muscles and slapped me up the side of the head with shaking chills, a high fever and a pounding headache. Since I was sitting in a restaurant celebrating a family birthday, this was an inconvenient time for me to get into an argument with a bug. Not wanting to spoil the party, I wrapped myself in the tablecloth, and hoped no one would notice. This was probably a 24-hour thing, I told myself. I'd feel better by tomorrow.

Day Two: I awoke, but began to wonder if I were dead. I couldn't be sure. There was a bright light shining in my face, and I felt disconnected from my body. With great effort, I wiggled

119

my big toe, then, my index finger. Finally, I managed to pry my parched lips open. Simultaneously, my husband flipped off the adjacent bathroom light, and I decided that yes, I was still alive. It was Sunday, of course, and it would have been easier to get an audience with the Queen of England than to see a doctor. But this was probably just one of those 36-hour things, I told myself. I'd feel better by tomorrow.

Day Three: I didn't feel better. There was nothing left to do but seek professional advice. Swaddled like a mummy, I shuffled off to the doctor's office. He shook his head, and said, "If only you had come in sooner." Apparently, a new drug is effective against Classic Flu, but only if you see a doctor and begin taking the pills within the first few hours of onset. Well, fat chance, I thought to myself, but I smiled sweetly instead, and asked what could be done now. Nothing was the answer I think I heard. Drink a lot of fluids. Take Tylenol. Endure. Be strong. Remember that I'm dealing with a classic here. Despite my doctor's diagnosis, however, I clung to the hope that this was only one of those 48-hour things. I'd be better by tomorrow.

Day Four: I discovered the Tylenol high, and felt a tinge of empathy for those sad souls addicted to OxyContin. I could see how it might have appeal. By spacing my Tylenol dosages in a precise pattern, I learned I could count on seventeen and a half minutes a day of up time. It was all about quality of life for me now. During those euphoric moments, I was convinced that this was not Classic Flu but only one of those 60-hour things. I'd be better by tomorrow.

Day Five: I grabbed paper tissues from the box by the handful. Let the trees die! Early on, I had plucked tissues one at a time from the container and had tried to use a tissue more than once. You know—I'd sort of worked around its four corners, as a good conservationist should. Now, I used three and four at a time. Still, ever the optimist, I thought this was probably one of those 72-hour things. I'd feel better tomorrow.

Day Six: As a perennial dieter, I've always felt a tad envious of the last meal served to prisoners on death row, and scripted my own menus in imagination. Now, I found myself in the unfamiliar position of having no appetite whatsoever. Apparently, Classic Flu attacks the taste buds and makes all food ranging from chocolate cake to fried fish taste like cardboard. Cardboard dipped in a chalk fondue to be precise. If this turned out to be only one of those 84-hour things, and my taste returned tomorrow, I vowed to eat an entire pie.

Day 12: I've come to understand that Classic Flu, like malaria, has the potential to linger for life. If it should sidle up to you, show proper respect. As for me, I'm organizing unilateral summit talks to discuss a peace treaty with Classic Flu. I'd like to feel a little better tomorrow.

Taser Gun Parties

I don't know who thought up the home party sales approach, but whoever it was had to be a genius. Cake, gossip and shopping—for a female it's the best of all worlds. Even if you're one of the rare women who does not enjoy these parties, who can decline an "invitation" from your next door neighbor or your husband's cousin?

The earliest ones I remember are the Stanley Parties in the early 1950s. Sometime during the Korean War, my mother went to a Stanley Party at Mable Dean's mom's house down the road, and famously bought the oven degreaser that my aunt later mistook for salad oil. Aunt Sis, who suffered from the early onset of cataracts that plagues our family, picked up Stanley's tall bottle of liquid cleanser to make her pink potato salad, and came close to sending our whole family to an early grave.

Stanley parties were passé by the 1960s, though, when Tupperware politely burped its way into the nation's living rooms. Amway was the rage in the 70s, and cosmetic parties put Mary Kaye into a pink Rolls Royce in the 80s. By the 1990s, *Southern Living* was selling home décor appropriately enough in the middle of our family rooms, and jewelry and candle parties were coming on strong.

But we're into a new century now, and women are not as shallow as we once were. The latest rage in direct marketing is the taser gun home party. I can't resist saying that I am stunned.

To be honest, I wasn't sure what a taser was until these party invitations started hitting mailboxes. Turns out it's a pocket size gun (it comes in pretty colors including metallic pink for the fashion conscious) loaded with compressed nitrogen. When the darts of nitrogen are released, a 50,000-volt jolt that can penetrate clothing immobilizes the target person. A recent party host was quoted in the media as saying "the guns are a must-have for women...If you know you are going to be in a certain situation where you might be uncomfortable, why not have it with you? It just makes you more confident."

I think she has a point. I've found myself in a lot of uncomfortable situations where 50,000-volt jolts would have come in handy. Last Sunday, for example, our minister preached until 12:15 when he knows good and well he's supposed to have the choir singing their last chords by 12 sharp. Perched on the hard church pew, my right hip was aching—pains were even shooting down to my big toe—and I was quite unconfident that I would be on time to meet our friends, as planned, for dinner. But, chalk it up to my haphazard planning, I didn't have a taser gun with me.

My gynecologist also comes to mind. I'm never comfortable when I see him for my annual exam, and don't even get me started on the technician he sends me to for a mammogram.

And since I'm being candid here, let me add that our three-year-old grandson Owen makes me uncomfortable dashing to the edge of precipices and climbing to the tippy-top of his world. I'd be a lot more confident around him if I could temporarily immobilize him.

The idea behind the taser gun parties, a company spokesman explained, is that women are more at ease purchasing defense equipment in someone's living room than in a storefront. I think this notion has possibilities that America's merchandisers have not even begun to plumb.

For example, I'm uncomfortable with the North Koreans and the Pakistani's having nuclear weapons. I'd be a lot more confident if had my own atom bomb in my purse since I know that I would only use it when absolutely necessary to maintain world peace and the balance of power. You know—to keep the world comfortable. (I trust my judgment on this more than all those crazy people running for president of the US of A.) Of course, I'd never dream of purchasing a bomb on the messy black market or even at a tacky strip mall. But if I could quietly pick up a bomb in my favorite color at a home party—while eating cake and gossiping too—well, there's a franchise opportunity waiting to explode.

Technology Bullies Me

I'm at the mercy of Technology's hard-drive heart, and it knows it. It taunts me as though I were a playground weakling. Despite success in other relationships, I lack the interpersonal skills necessary to live in peace with the mega-bytes, sensor eyes, and automated-everythings that now run the world. In the spirit of the 21st century, I've looked around for someone to blame, and I've homed in on my maternal grandfather, George Hudson.

I adored Gran, and he could talk anybody out of their socks, but he couldn't communicate with machines. Their soulless innards were as mysterious to him as the dark side of the moon. He could barely drive a car. When something stopped working, even something as simple as a blown fuse in the fuse box, Gran would wave a piece of baling wire in the air—the duct tape of his universe—and send up a prayer that life would hold together. It's a wonder the man didn't get electrocuted.

I have this notion of a recessive unable-to-make-things-work gene being handed down to Gran and me from some shivering ancestor who failed to coax fire from a flint stone. I figure that's how our talking gene got rolling. Our freezing to death progenitor had to talk fast to convince someone else to start a fire for him.

But neither Gran nor my caveman forbear lived in my postmodern world where even going to the restroom is a technological mine field. Today's comfort station is enough to make a grown woman weep.

I've spent as long as fifteen minutes in public places trying to convince the commode that, yes, I really am ready to exit now, and it's time for your wherever it may be sensor to do what

124

it does best and flush. I've been reduced to begging, standing up and sitting down, and jumping from side to side. Can you imagine how ridiculous a woman my age looks waving her arms over her head in a tiny toilet cubicle? It's a wonder I haven't been arrested for solicitation like that senator from Idaho whose foot slipped over the line in an airport stall.

The new fangled lavatory faucets humiliate me too. They fall into two general categories: the ones with no handles and the kind that you forcibly hold in the on position with one hand while washing the other hand. The latter baffles me completely. I have no idea how to wash a single hand without help from the other. It is, after all, called washing your hands not washing your hand. All you can do when you run into these contraptions is pray you have a forgotten, crunched up dry-wipe packet hiding in your purse.

But I keep thinking I could master the faucets with no handles at all. I see others succeed in enticing water to flow voluntarily from these hoity-toity sculptures, so why can't I? Apparently you're supposed to hold your hands in an exact formation, at an invisible but tightly defined spot in thin air. But there are no instructions, I keep insisting! What is the magical latitude and longitude that will make the water gush?

Now the soap dispensers are getting in on the act and are demanding a little hand-hula routine before they will consent to part with a tiny, measured amount of soap. "Look," I tried explaining to one especially stingy soap do-dad, "if you knew where these hands have been you would give me more than one squirt without my even having to ask." Because where they had been, I could have gone on, was all over the toilet stall trying to locate a manual button to flush the commode.

Then there are the parsimonious paper towel dispensers that also demand a magic word to release a helpful scrap. "Open sesame, open sesame" I chant to no effect.

Oh, I could go on and on. I did, however, resolve my issues with the TV remote that's programmed in Chinese. I leave the TV on 24/7 now and mute the volume. Hey, even weaklings win some battles.

In Memory of Thanksgiving

NEWS BULLETIN— Unidentified sources report that Thanksgiving, an apparent target in the world-wide Economic War, was killed in a hit and run incident on Main Street, USA, on or about November 1. Hired mercenaries were seen rolling over her as they roared from the east coast to the west wrapping all of America in artificial garland and red ribbon. Thanksgiving, well known for her peaceful political philosophy, is said to have courageously clung to life. She was seen waving her leaf-stenciled banners from city lampposts in non-violent resistance until her final moments. The official cause of death is thought to be aspiration of plastic holly berries made in China that were floating in the tailwind of the assassins.

Thanksgiving was preceded in death by her Grandmothers who lived over the meadow and through the woods; her Mother, the archetypical, stalwart woman who emigrated to America on the Mayflower; her father, Governor William Bradford, who invited all the neighbors in for a grand feast to celebrate her birth in 1621; her husband, Bah Humbug, who liked to eat pumpkin pie but did not like to shop; her sister, Priscilla Alden, made famous in William Wadsworth Longfellow's *New York Times* best-seller *The Courtship of Miles Standish*; a cousin, Sarah Joespha Hale, who successfully campaigned to make Thanksgiving's birthday a national holiday in 1863 (Sarah is also remembered for her composition of "Mary Had A Little Lamb"); several Daughters and Sons who did not put up a Christmas tree until the calendar said it was December 1; and an uncle, Ebenezer Scrooge. Thanksgiving is survived by a host of Turkeys.

Due to scheduling conflicts throughout the Holiday Season, there will be no funeral services. Memorial gifts may be made to the Martha Stewart Foundation or to Williams and Sonoma who lovingly cared for Thanksgiving during her last frail years of life.

Georgia Green Stamper of Lexington, Kentucky, is organizing a communal sigh at midnight tonight to honor the legacy of the deceased holiday. Stamper urges Americans of all faiths to set their tables with leaf-shaped placemats which can be purchased at Walmart, light candles that are molded into little Pilgrim figures, and remember together Thanksgiving's slow, elegant stroll through the gray Novembers of yesteryear. Stamper says that Thanksgiving will be missed by all who loved her.

In loving memory of Thanksgiving,
born 1621—died 2012

New Year's Eve

Bing Crosby may have dreamed of snow, but my Christmases in the Bluegrass have been mostly muddy, and have been better for it, in my opinion. I have, however, been stuck in a blizzard with a blind date on New Year's Eve. Because of that singular experience, New Year's is painted forever white in my memory.

My parents and I, along with several ancient relatives, had been invited to a holiday dinner at the home of my G-Uncle Murf Hudson, Aunt Bessie, and their teenage son James. They lived near Dry Ridge about 20 miles north of our Owen County farm, and the weather was okay on our late afternoon trip to their place. I mention this to emphasize that blizzards, like the storms in life, can catch us by surprise.

I looked forward to the evening because I adored my cousin James. He, like me, was an only child, having come into his parents' lives deep into their middle age. He and I substituted for the siblings neither of us had. A few years older than me, he had movie star good looks (I told people he was kin to Rock Hudson and they believed me) and he was—still is—one of the funniest people I've ever known. Already my ideal big brother, he now had the aura of a college freshman and had acquired a beautiful girlfriend.

When we arrived, he pulled me aside.

"I've promised Sally I'll take her to Cincinnati to the movies and to walk around Fountain Square at midnight to see the lights and hear the bells ring in the New Year. If your parents will let you go, my buddy Gary* says he'll come along and we'll make it a double date."

My heart skipped. I was fifteen and a half, and my hottest date thus far had been sitting by a boy at church. Was it possible the life I'd envisioned might be about to begin?

To my surprise, my parents said I could go. Perhaps they knew that my old-fashioned aunt and uncle, nearly a generation older than them, wouldn't let James out of the house unless I went too, and Mother and Daddy would've understood the importance of a New Years Eve date to an eighteen year old boy. They also trusted James to take care of me.

As soon as dinner was over, he and I slipped out, making our get-away before our parents noticed it had started to snow a little. By the time we reached Sally's house two miles south in Williamstown, the roads were white. Like us, she hurried out before her parents could say no. We then drove five miles north to Gary's house in Dry Ridge.

Gary, tall and lanky, climbed into the car and I thought my prayers were answered. He looked like Buddy Holly with a flattop in his dark framed glasses, navy blazer and skinny tie. I tried not to giggle when we were introduced. Gary—a college freshman like James—was not impressed by me, however. A year or so later and his reaction might have been different, but on that fateful night I looked every awkward minute of my fifteen and a half years. After a polite hello, he didn't say another word to me the entire evening. I spent the night worrying that James had paid Gary to go out with me.

By this time deep footprints were tracking in the fresh snow, and James nixed the trip to Cincinnati and opted to go to the drive-in theater at Dry Ridge. This was disappointing, but I figured it was still more glamorous than welcoming the New Year with the ancients and Guy Lombardo on TV.

The first clue that we were in trouble should have been the vacant lot at the drive-in. If there was another car there I don't remember it. Within thirty minutes of our arrival, we were in a whiteout, unable to see the giant screen much less the movie. James attempted some self-deprecating wit about our exciting New Years Eve, but Gary was mostly silent. Finally, the guys decided they'd better get out and evaluate our situation. They stepped out of the car—and vanished into a drift. That's when I got scared. We needed to get home.

Gary volunteered to push the car out of the drift while James steered and accelerated. That flailing effort produced nothing more than the odor of burnt tire rubber. Then, in a surreal frenzy, they both began to shove the car like madmen. After an eternity, it budged. With visibility near zero, we set out for Gary's house because it was the closest.

By the grace of God we found our way through the blinding snow to Gary's basement garage. I offered up a silent prayer of thanks that we were still alive while the guys began putting snow chains on the tires to get us home. Alas, neither of them had ever done this before, and the complicated process was slow and noisy. I'm also guessing they didn't ask permission to borrow the chains from Gary's dad. Anywise, he stomped down to the basement after a while and threw a full-fledged temper tantrum in our direction replete with wild hand gyrations to punctuate the tirade.

James and I came from quiet families, and we'd never seen an adult pitch a fit like that, much less at us. And to this day, I have no idea what the man expected us to do. I don't recall his inviting us to spend the night, or even offering us a cup of hot chocolate or the use of the bathroom. At that point I decided I didn't care if Gary didn't like me. His dad was not appropriate grandfather material.

That's when I began to laugh. And then James did too. Sally and Gary looked at us like we were crazy, but we couldn't stop. We laughed and laughed and laughed even though we knew we probably shouldn't.

Eventually the chains snapped on, and we got back to James' house in one piece, though my family couldn't get home to Owen County until the next day. James and Sally broke up not long afterwards, and I never laid eyes on Gary again.

This is not a holiday memory that would inspire Bing Crosby to dream and sing, but real life is, after all, more like an abstract painting than a Currier and Ives engraving. We stared at the New Year in a whiteout, uncertain of our way forward—but who, I ask now, can ever see into the future with clarity? We made it through, however, and even laughed.

* Of course, Gary's name has been changed.

130

To Every Thing
There Is A Season

prologue iii ...

to every thing there is a season

To every thing there is a season, and a time to every purpose
under the heaven: A time to be born, and a time to die; a time
to plant, and time to pluck up that which is planted; . . . A time
to weep, and a time to laugh; a time to mourn, and a time to
dance;
— Ecclesiastes 3: 1-2, 4

The passing seasons meant more than a change of wardrobe to
my parents' life on the farm. Each month of the year arrived
with specific responsibilities to the land that needed to be tended
to then, neither sooner nor later. Now, in my urban climate-
controlled home, I mark the calendar by switching the wreath on
my front door and the variety of flora by the steps. Though it
matters little, I do this as though I were obliged to obey some
primeval instinct handed down to me by hunter-gatherer for-
bears. My city neighbors do the same, and I wonder if we follow
these rituals to remind ourselves—if only subliminally—of our
race's ancient wisdom, never expressed better than in Ecclesiastes.

My father died in a January rain. His tractor slipped on the
hill behind the Old Barn, and did not stop sliding until it overturned in the bottoms below. Time stopped, suspended in that
moment, although Mother and I busied ourselves with the
business of death.

I watched in silence as the January earth froze and squeezed
all hope out of the crocus, the hyacinths and daffodils. Febru-

ary's ice storm finished the massacre. And then one day I looked up and saw that the flowers had not only survived my winter doubts, but were thriving under an April sun. Oh, winter came back around again, of course. It always does. But so does spring—and summer and fall.

Dicksie

In Nebraska this week, it's colder than at the North Pole. In Florida, the temperatures dipped below freezing. Here in Kentucky, life lies dormant in the frozen ground covered by snow. The naked trees reach their thin arms toward the heavens like a forest of Holocaust victims pleading for help. It's January, the duplicitous month, named for the two faced Roman god Janus who looked backward and forward at the same time

And Ernie and I begin the New Year, the new decade, saying good-bye to one who has traveled with him from the beginning of memory. Word has come that his vibrant cousin, Dicksie Stamper Bradford, has died from complications of pneumonia after the onset of a winter virus. In the 21st century, women in middle age, at least women close to my age, are not supposed to die from things like this. Our emotions run the gamut from anger to disbelief. We remind ourselves, however, that Dicksie didn't waste much time in life, and it follows that she would handle death in the same efficient manner.

Dicksie's story is extraordinary in the way ordinary lives can be. She married her high school sweetheart, raised a son, doted on a grandchild, and worked nearly every day of her life. After retiring from her job with Kentucky state government, she began a second career as a licensed real estate agent. Finally, in the last few years, she and Billy had escaped to Florida where she was having a ball raising orchids and fishing.

It's impossible to remember Dicksie without using the word pretty. On her mother's side she was a granddaughter of Noble Nash Hundley, the colorful Kentucky River steamboat pilot, and she inherited the physical good looks that marked his tribe, evenly proportioned features, flawless skin. The Stampers, though, took credit for her blue eyes. Dicksie also brought prettiness into the things she did, like the music she made on the organ at her church year after year, and her flair for decorating her home. Turning thrift store finds into treasures, using paint and imagination, her houses, wherever she landed, were always modest showplaces, and of course, spotless. Dicksie's middle name was Clean.

Dicksie's father and Ernie's dad were brothers. She was only eight months older than Ernie, but early on she assumed the role of his older sister, in part because he had no siblings, but mostly because she played this role for just about everyone in her sprawling family. She and Ernie were among the last Owen Countians—among the last Kentuckians—to attend a one-room school, and their aunt, Georgia Belle Stamper Giles, was their teacher at Gratz Elementary. I think about half of the 20 students in grades one through eight were first cousins, and those who weren't related were informally adopted into the Stamper clan. Perhaps this unique early experience that interwove family-school-community fostered the sense of responsibility Dicksie had for any who were her kin.

There are many stories that could be told, but many of them are not mine to tell. I do know that she stuck up for Ernie when they were children, and stuck with him throughout his life. If you were family, Dicksie was there when you were sick, helped pick you up when you were down and out, and celebrated with you when you succeeded.

It's appropriate then that her last gift to the family was an extraordinary weekend reunion this past September. The first generation of Stamper cousins are scattered in age across three decades and are splintered geographically. One lives in California, another in New York, a few in Ohio and Indiana, Dicksie in Florida, and the others here and there across Kentucky. They aren't a homogeneous group, either, despite their common DNA. Some are ardent Democrats, others staunch Republicans, and their occupations are as varied as the "butcher, baker, candlestick maker" in the old nursery rhyme. In the 42 years we've been married, there had been only two previous reunions, the last one 20 years ago.

Undaunted, Dicksie set a date a year in advance, booked space at Butler State Park Lodge, and began summoning the clan to gather. Ernie and I were uncertain if many would show up, but Dicksie proceeded on the "Field of Dreams" theory. If you build it they will come.

And come they did, even unto the fourth generation. Some arrived on Friday night, setting the tone for the weekend with marathon card games in the lobby and conversations that lasted until midnight. Others arrived in time for lunch on Saturday, and by Saturday night's dinner, the group was 60 strong, spilling out of the private banquet room into the lodge's main dining hall.

At first, we didn't know each other. Conversations began with "my father or grandfather was—" But soon we were reminiscing, checking facts and dates, pouring over family photographs. From there we went on to share our own life stories, our opinions on politics and the economy, and our worries about the grandchildren. Most important of all, old wounds were healed, most hatchets of discord buried. When we left on Sunday morning, we were a family.

Throughout the weekend, Dicksie was our queen bee, presiding with dignity over this event she had organized down to the nuts on the table. When news came of her death, I couldn't help but think of Tom Sawyer, who attended his own funeral in one of the most memorable scenes in American literature. Like Tom, Dicksie got to see us all gathered together in one place, and know, really know, that we loved her.

There are lessons to be learned from any life, and Dicksie's, like everyone else's, was not without its valleys. But her death reminds me to look forward this cold January day. After all, "if Winter comes," the poet wrote, "can Spring be far behind?"

The Garbage Collectors

The sound of a rough motor blasted against my winter bedroom window. My sleep-drugged brain struggled to make sense of the noise. It was pitch dark, the middle of the night. Would burglars be that loud? Should I wake my husband and prod him to investigate? (Like Dagwood's Blondie, I've taken that role in our self-defense throughout forty-plus years of marriage.) Then the ping and clang of garbage cans echoed up and down our street, and my mind shifted into gear.

On Tuesdays, before daybreak, nameless, faceless people come through our neighborhood emptying trashcans for the city's taxpayers. It was not the middle of the night as I had thought, but with temperatures hovering at seven degrees Fahrenheit at 5:30 on a January morning, I thought the garbage folks might think that a subtle distinction.

I pulled the comforter over my head, determined to sleep until our retirement alarm clock went off at seven a.m., and said a little thank you to whoever might be listening that garbage hauling was not my job. I wondered how early they'd left their beds to reach the city's central garage to then drive the big city truck to our outlying sub-division before dawn. At least by four a.m., I decided. That would allow them time for hot coffee and a quick breakfast, but maybe not a shower. Probably they shave and bathe when their shift is over, I concluded, and that would save a few minutes in the morning. Still, I speculated they seldom stayed up for the guilty pleasure of watching Leno or Letterman after the eleven o'clock news.

I've never been a willing morning person unless staying up until one or two a.m. to read a novel counts as morning and not night. I never got the magic of sunrise, despite growing up on a

138

farm where work for the grown-ups began when the rooster crowed. My childhood friend, Judy Kaye Glass, says her earliest memories of me are my racing to catch the school bus with breakfast clutched in my hands. I always overslept, she recalls.

Thus, I've ever been grateful to those who are willing to get up in the wee hours to keep society functioning. I think of those in the medical community—doctors, nurses, technicians and support staff. I think of bus drivers and policemen, newscasters and the third shift at factories. The list goes on and on.

But this morning I am fixed on the garbage collectors. Given their somewhat unpleasant work—performed outside in all sorts of weather—I wonder what tricks they utilize to get their bodies out of bed. Maybe they go to sleep at eight p.m. Or maybe their alarm clock sounds like a fire engine's siren blasting in their ear. More likely, the prospect of a decent paycheck at the end of the pay period is their strongest motivator, and I can understand that the faces of my children needing food and shelter would nudge even my lazy bones up before the sun.

Suddenly I remember that Martin Luther King Jr.—whose birthday gives many a chance to sleep-in at least once in gloomy January—was in Memphis to support the garbage workers' strike when he was murdered. With embarrassment, I realize I have no idea how or when that strike was resolved. The Memphis garbage workers' strike is simply a footnote in history to me surrounding an awful event.

I'm sorry I wasn't paying attention, I say to anyone who might be listening. And then I roll over for another hour of sleep.

Bill and Me

The snow finally arrived early this morning. It's a measly three inches, but it's better than nothing. I don't know who is more relieved to see it—me or Bill, the nice weatherman on channel 18.

As for myself, I was afraid we'd eat through our extra provisions before the storm arrived. When Bill first sang out his alarm three days ago, I dashed to one of the three mega-markets a half mile down the road to load up our larder. Since the sun was shining, I didn't even take time to throw on a coat because I could tell from the sound of Bill's voice that this was going to be a big one, maybe a monster. Almost running through the aisles, I grabbed the essentials to sustain life: potato chips, doughnuts, granola bars, Cheetos, anything that doesn't have to be cooked. Oh, and because I'm trying to lose weight, a lot of Diet Pepsi.

Back home, I began my three day, hour-to-hour, vigil along with Bill. He tried to stay cheerful, laughing and smiling every time he popped up on our HD screen, but I could tell he was rattled as the hours stretched into days and no flakes dropped from the heavens. To be honest, I began to lose faith, and fretted that I'd eaten my allotted Weight Watchers points forward through the month of May in vain.

Bill, I think, has been worried about keeping his job. I wouldn't be one bit surprised if management has given him a warning: whip us up a fine winter storm, Bill, or get lost. "Who needs a TV weatherman if the weather is always fair?" I can hear those budget-cutting miscreants grousing.

And poor Bill. At the last moment, one approaching storm after another has jagged north to Ohio or south to Tennessee, or to Eastern or Western Kentucky, and skipped right over us folks in Lexington. As he apologized to viewers last night, he explained that he's like a surgeon. He can get us prepped for surgery, get the operating room ready, the scalpel sterilized, the gauze at hand, but if the patient dies before the operation, there is nothing more he can do.

Bill loves a good storm more than anybody I ever saw. If it doesn't kill people that is—Bill doesn't have a mean bone in him. Actually, his enthusiasm for aberrant weather strikes an evangelistic chord. I truly believe he wants to save the world from the whims of nature.

He's young enough to be my son, and that's a shame, because I think he would have soared to stardom—maybe won a Nobel Peace Prize—if he had lived through the kind of winters we used to have before all this global warming got started, back when men were men, and the county couldn't afford snowplows.

In the winter of 1976-77, we were living in Ashland in a cold house that sat about two miles from the Ohio River. I had a four year old, a two year old, and was expecting our third child in March. Cynics may say that my personal circumstances have exaggerated my memory of that winter, but I beg to differ. According to the people who keep track of these things, the snowfall that December, January, and February was twice the annual average. The snow came to a crescendo near the end of January when the Ohio River Valley was hit with the tail end of a blizzard straight out of Buffalo.

But it wasn't the snow that stopped us in '76-'77—it was the cold that wouldn't let any of it melt. December's first snowflake was still with us when the spring thaw came. The thermometer bottomed out in mid-January at minus 25 degrees Fahrenheit, and the Ohio River froze solid. The bold walked from one shore to the other. The timid stayed inside wrapped in quilts and coached their husbands on how to deliver a baby "just in case."

We didn't think the next winter could get any worse here, but it did. In January, 1978, nearby Cincinnati was hit with a jaw-dropping 46 inches of snow, and upriver in Ashland we had about the same amount. But every part of Kentucky got at least 23 inches of snow that month according to records kept by the state climatologist, Glenn Conner. Early February dumped 11 more inches on the region.

141

Hemmed in for weeks at a time with an infant and two small children, I decided one desperate day to bundle up the kids and walk to my next door neighbor's house for coffee and human companionship. The Donner Pass would not have looked more treacherous to me as I ventured out into the tunnel, high as my head, that Ernie had carved out with a shovel to connect our front door to what might be left of civilization.

We'd made it to what vaguely looked like the street, when one of the girls took a step off course and vanished from sight. Somehow, juggling an infant in one arm and frantically pulling and digging with the other, I rescued the child before frostbite set in. We hurried back into our cave and didn't venture out again until the bears told us the flowers were blooming.

Bill would've gotten a kick out of those Kentucky winters in the seventies. He's a man born too late to fulfill his destiny.

Birthday Dinner

I've blown through another birthday this week, but I've reached an age where these milestones are bittersweet. I'm thrilled to be having another one because as I watch one dear friend after another struggle with unexpected disease and loss, I understand in an intimate, new way that life is fragile.

And I am greedy. Even should I live to be 101 like Uncle Bo, I will covet more time. I'll beg for one more April filled to the edge of the sky with white blossoms on the pear trees, and rabbits munching daffodils in the backyard garden.

This birthday, though, was special, and will be forever framed in my memory. The newest member of our family, our son-in-law John, is a master chef at the grill, and he stepped forward to prepare a sumptuous feast for me and other family members at his and our daughter's home. They've been married for only two and a half months, and this first official family celebration around their table was important in ways perhaps only adult children and their parents can appreciate. The stage was set with candlelight and porcelain china, perfect lemon chicken, fresh asparagus and squash, wild rice, hot yeast rolls— but the play was not about food.

It was about the construction of a new family paradigm. Our eldest daughter Shan, in her mid-thirties, is the last of our three children to marry, and John, also in his mid-thirties, has joined our story at the halfway point. There is catching up to do, and we swamp him with our history and photographs and inside family jokes until his eyes politely glaze over.

John is an only child, never before married, and I have a rush of empathy for him as I think how strange it may be for him of a sudden to have two sisters-in-law bookended by two brothers-in-law, two nieces and two nephews at varying stages of civilization, not to mention a spare set of parents in Ernie and me. John is gracious to a fault, embracing us with love and good humor, insisting a large family is what he always dreamed of having. And yet I understand that it is the history we will share together that will ultimately make us family.

Our first son-in-law, Tim, was not quite twenty when he started coming around to visit our middle daughter. Now we are thirteen years, three babies, and a few gray hairs down the road. We've helped each other pack up and move multiple times— we've lived in three different houses since we met Tim, and he and Becky have lived in five. Together, we've walked the floor with screaming newborns who would not sleep, and donned masks to tiptoe into a neonatal ICU unit to pray over an oxygen tent. We've weathered surgeries in their household and ours. We've cheered Tim's business success, and encouraged him in difficult times. There have been bushels of ordinary days, too, grilling hamburgers, ordering pizza, watching ballgames on TV, talking about books or dissecting the news. And Tim made my mother laugh, and wept when he carried her to her grave. We've watched Tim grow up to become a fine man. He's watched us grow older.

Alex was in his mid-twenties when he and our youngest daughter, Georgeann, met about seven years ago. In his next to last year of medical school, he was already near a doctor and so very smart—and yet he was still so young. He's come to us with earnest questions about mortgages and rain gutters, taxes and insurance, flowering shrubs and grass—things they don't teach in school. We've watched movies together and shared novels we admired. And then one night there came the phone call that Georgeann had gone into labor three months too early, and we arrived at their house to find Alex waiting for us at the front door, crying. Through the long summer of fear and bed-rest that followed, we watched him tenderly care for our daughter, waiting on her, entertaining her so she would not go stir crazy, holding her hand then furtively checking her pulse a dozen or more times a day. We've watched him become a doting and protective father, a man in the fullest meaning of the word.

As we sat around John and Shan's birthday table the other night, I thought about the family members who had hovered about me when I was born. Though a few remain, most are gone. Mawmaw and Pawpaw Green who rode a Greyhound bus fifty miles to visit Mother and me in a Covington hospital. Gran Hudson who arrived in an ambulance he'd hired from Rogers Funeral Home to escort Mother and me back to his house—where he fed us and cared for us and rocked me for months until Daddy came home from the war. Aunt Rose and Uncle Gip who drove Mother to the hospital and waited with her until I was here, who telegraphed my father to tell him "Jerri and baby girl both doing fine." Daddy, and Mother too, are gone now.

But their kind ghosts sit at the table with me still, and so I introduce them to John. I tell them how much I like him. I tell them I think he's come to stay.

Number Six

Bonk, bonk, bonk.

"What's that sound?" Ernie bolted up in bed and fumbled for the alarm clock.

"What time is it?" I mumbled, and where was I? I was pretty sure I wasn't home. Maybe in a hotel room?

"A tornado warning!" I said it out loud the moment the thought registered in my brain. I could hear rain slapping at the windows, looking for trouble.

"No, the phone," Ernie said, and then he was out of bed searching for his new iPhone that signals incoming calls with a clever bonk instead of a ring or a song.

I sat straight up in bed, wide-awake now. In my crowd, no one has ever rung me up after midnight to invite me to lunch. Sometimes, a bewildered soul has dialed the wrong number, or a teenage prankster has gone on the loose. And half-asleep, I've picked up a phone more than once in my life to hear a twisted mind pounce on me with obscenities. Nine times out of ten, though, a ringing phone in the wee hours means an SOS call from someone I love.

That possibility woke me up. This was no hotel room, I realized. I was in Indianapolis in a guest room bed where I'd been sleeping for the past month. Our middle daughter Becky was recuperating from a serious surgery, and she'd asked me to play the role of Alice in her family's production of "The Brady Bunch."

Now our oldest daughter, Shan, was calling from a Kentucky hospital. She'd gone into labor almost three weeks early, and yes, she was confident this was not a false alarm.

146

Shan and her husband John are not Abraham and Sarah, but they were half-way through their thirties when they married. When several years passed with no announcement, Ernie and I assumed that they would not be having children. When Shan told us last July that she was pregnant, we were surprised—and overjoyed.

The pregnancy proceeded without problems, and Shan, an attorney, was still working every day. And so, though it sounds silly to admit, we were taken off guard when the baby decided to enter the world a few weeks early. We think now that she didn't want to miss March Madness. She descends from a long line of UK basketball fanatics—her mother among them—and she had a good old time rooting the Wildcats to the NCAA Final Four during her first few weeks of life.

"We've got to leave for Lexington," one, then both, of us said. And so we did that. We jumped out of bed, brushed our teeth and dressed, gathered a month's worth of possessions scattered around the house, woke up Becky and her family to say good-bye, and headed south on I-65 in the slickest, blackest night I've ever seen.

I prayed at every mile marker. I prayed that the baby would be all right. I prayed that Shan would be okay. I prayed that Ernie wouldn't doze and skid off the highway. And though I felt a little sheepish, I prayed that we would make it to Lexington before the baby was born.

As it turned out, we arrived long before she did because more drama lay ahead. After nine hours of labor, somebody realized she was trying to come into the world upside down. I could rant here about the mysteries of modern medicine—I mean don't they have ways to know this stuff nowadays—but all's well that ends well. Shan had an emergency C-section and both mother and baby did fine.

And so after a cold, harsh winter, the youngest of our six grandchildren arrived with the crocus and daffodils in March. She's laughed like the springtime ever since, one of the happiest babies I've ever known. I like to think she's delighted with her start in life because her parents gave her a used name, Georgia Jane, for both her grandmothers.

Now there are those who think a girl will never get elected to the Homecoming Court if she doesn't have a trendy name favored by movie stars and pop singers. Others think a child cannot find her own way in the world unless she has a name invented for her, that no one else who has ever lived has owned. But I think a used name can anchor you and help you feel a little less alone in this world.

I know something about sharing a name with older relatives. In my family there's a Georgia under every other rock, and I admit that it gets confusing. And when she's about fifteen, I could tell her, a name like Georgia Jane will sound old-fashioned, as out of style as a flapper's dress or leg-o-mutton sleeves, and she'll consider changing it to Peppi with an i.

I would remind her then that her DNA has a smidgen of all of us who have preceded her, and, if she'll overlook our flaws and embrace our strengths, we have a lot to give her. We've done it all before her, for her. She only has to ask.

On behalf of all the Georgias, I'd tell her about the three generations of my Grandmother Hudson's family who got this Georgia thing rolling. I'd urge her to claim their graciousness and charm—charisma some might call it now, but it was more than that, something fundamental within their being. Oh, and she shouldn't overlook their skill in the kitchen. Their legendary angel biscuits come to mind.

On the Stamper side, I'd remind her of her G-G-Aunt Georgia Belle Stamper Giles. She taught in a one-room school for a lifetime, laughed at something every day, spent twenty years getting her college degree one course at a time, and went wading in the ocean for the first time when she was eighty-three. A passion for education, a good sense of humor and grit is a formula for happiness that's hard to beat.

Look to my Aunt Georgia Green for godliness and longevity. She married Daddy's brother, my Uncle Woodrow, and so technically I'm not biologically related to her, but her kindness claims me as her own. Still going strong at 95, she may be too good to die.

From my grandfather George Hudson—not a Georgia but close enough—look to his good head for business. More importantly, I'd remind her of his willingness to feed anyone in need who came to his door, and his devotion to family. If you were kin to Gran Hudson, he stood by you even if you were not as good as you should have been, even when your days were more often thin than thick.

I'd ask, too, for a spirit as wise as her Aunt Georgia Ann's—her mother's sister—and her determination to do her best at everything she attempts.

But what, I wonder, do I have to give her? Is a passion for words a good enough gift? Maybe. Maybe the stories of who we Georgia's have been, or hoped to be, or what we have lost, and what we have seen, will make a difference in the way Georgia Jane shapes her story. Whether they do or not, I give them to her, along with my name, with love. Love makes this journey through life easier, I've learned, whatever your name may be.

When Your Babies Become Mothers

Mother's Day is just past, and my sweet girls have done for me what good daughters do on such holidays. And yet, I feel as though I should be the one celebrating them. I'm semi-retired. They're still on the frontlines of active duty.

Becky slid into the weekend with all three of her children down with the croup, a husband out of town on a business trip, and a puppy that's not housebroken. She reported she'd spent much of the week in a steaming shower trying to keep the kids breathing—when she wasn't outside with the children's dog who has both a nervous bladder and nervous intestines. When she opened up her email and found the Chucky Cheese mouse wishing her "Happy Mother's Day!" and offering her discount coupons to celebrate "her day" with the mouse, she broke down and cried.

Georgeann's week wasn't much easier. Her three-year-old Annelise went from playing happily on the floor at six p.m. to the hospital emergency room with double pneumonia by 10 p.m. Baby Hudson, now thirteen months, decided to get in on the act, and came down with an ear infection two days later.

Hudson also doesn't care that he's supposed to be sleeping through the night, pointing, or saying x number of words by now. He isn't at all impressed with his mother's exhaustion, her angst, or her umpteen degrees in psychology. Annelise, on the other hand, may already have gotten a PhD. on the sly. She recently asked her mother if the Sleep Fairy would bring her an iPad if she slept through the night in her own bed.

And then Becky's five year old Owen sent her into Mother-hood's Hall of Despair by asking nonchalantly if **!* was a better word than love. That may have been the same day that sweet Eliza bloodied her brother Jared's nose for going one teasing taunt too far. Oh—and eleven year old Jared is not too fond of showers, brushing his teeth, or vegetables. Is that normal, Becky asks me?

To be honest, watching my babies have babies is sort of like seeing the movie version of a favorite book I've read. It's kind of the same, and yet it feels like a different story. Perhaps that's because I don't play the same role in the movie as I did in the book.

Olan Mills Photography

Georgia's Daughters: Becky, Shan, and Baby Georgeann

And then of course real life is not fiction, and the plot twists are not always logical, justified, or neatly resolved. That has been the hardest thing I've had to do as a mother—explain to my adult daughters that this mothering gig is unpredictable, that effort does not equal a guaranteed result.

With the exception of the Virgin Mary, no one is good enough to be a mother, I go on to tell them, and I never met a child who understood from the get-go that he/she had an obligation to be normal, to do things in a certain way, at a certain time, in response to certain parenting techniques.

Unless, of course, normal is something that upsets grown-ups. Like eleven-year-old boys who dislike showers. Siblings who tease and quarrel with each other. Three-year-olds who won't stay in their own beds till morning. Little boys who learn to shock their elders with naughty words. One-year-olds who won't sleep through the night.

It is, however, normal for a mom to get weepy or grouchy when she hasn't had a full night's sleep in a year. I'd also tell them I suspect every mother yells at her child at least once in a lifetime, if she's honest. It's also normal to have fantasies of running away to a hotel room—not for a tryst—but to sleep, and watch TV and read, and have meals delivered by room service.

I would not tell them that their best efforts do not matter—because, oh, they do, they do. But I would remind them that a good story often has a lot of turns in the plot.

I would tell them I can see that they love their babies to the core, as intensely as I loved mine, and that most of the time that pulls us good-enough mothers through to a happy ending.

I would wish them a Happy Mother's Day—and a good night's sleep.

Memorial Day

Yesterday, Memorial Day, I stood at the graves of my great-grandfather, John William Green, and his brother Joseph, who fought for the Confederate States of America in the Civil War. Unlike Veterans' Day, full of parades and medals and ceremonies, Memorial Day is mostly about cemeteries, seems to me. No wonder Americans have turned it into a national picnic celebrating the arrival of summer. Otherwise, it would be the most depressing day of the year. Conceived in grief, birthed in our nation's anguish, Memorial Day is the child of the Civil War, reminding us that war is, after all, about blood sweat and tears, whether one is right or wrong, wins or loses.

Johnny and Joe Green both managed to get back home to Owen County after the war, albeit with tuberculosis and other wounds to the soul. Their brother, George W. Green, with the "grey eyes, fair complexion," did not. He died in a Military Hospital at Rye Cove, and lies, I presume, in an unmarked grave in a Virginia field. How am I to feel about their sacrifice? I've long since given up trying to understand why poor Kentucky farm boys like the Green brothers gave their all to split the country in half.

In an undated daguerreotype, the only picture of him that survives, my John William has a merry look on his face. I wonder if he is the source of the Green family's famous sense of humor, and I realize I've heard no stories about him. I know only that he lived through the war to die of consumption when my Pawpaw Green was eight years old. All of his children, including my grandfather, were born after his surrender and pardon at the end of the war. That's justification enough in my opinion for our annual family picnic on Memorial Day weekend.

153

John William Green

A number of towns across the nation, from the Deep South to the northeast, claim the distinction of holding the first Memorial Day ceremony, and there seems little doubt that spontaneous observations did occur in multiple places about the same time at the end of the Civil War. I've read various stories about these early Memorial Day events, but the two I like best are these because they focus on healing the wounds of war.

On May 5, 1868, three years after the Civil War ended, the first "Decoration Day" observance was held in Arlington National Cemetery on the veranda of Confederate General Robert E. Lee's family home, Arlington. Union General and Mrs. Ulysses S. Grant presided. The U. S. Veterans Department's website says, "After speeches, children from the Soldiers' and Sailors' Orphan Home and members of the GAR made their way through the cemetery, strewing flowers on both Union and Confederate graves, reciting prayers and singing hymns."

Two years earlier, on April 25, 1866, a group of women in Columbus, Mississippi, had gone to the cemetery where the many Confederate soldiers who died in the Battle of Shiloh were buried. They went with flowers to decorate the Confederate graves, but were so moved by the nearby neglected graves of the fallen Union soldiers, they decorated those, too. I think that is a beautiful story, even more impressive than the later ceremonial one at Arlington, because it surely must have been spontaneous and genuine, and was offered up by women who knew the harshness and divisiveness of the Civil War firsthand.

If we must have wars, as it seems we are doomed to endure until the end of time, let us then continue to have Marshall Plans in peacetime—at least old women and children strewing flowers on both friend and foe.

And let us have picnics, too, I thought, as I bent to place a red rose on Private John William Green's grave.

County Fair

Before Disney World. Before Six Flags Over Every City in America. Before the glitzy arcade in the mega-mall. Before all of that, there was the county fair. It exploded like the Fourth of July in the long stillness of my childhood summers and whirled my heart on the merry-go-round until I was drunk with exhilaration. I raced the painted wooden ponies as high as the sky.

Daddy served on the Fair Board for decades, and the annual event was a holiday for us, a break from the intense seasonal work on the farm. Though the merry-go-round never lost its magic for me, when I got older, about twelve, the fair became the apex of my summer social life. Country miles separated me from my classmates, and I didn't see many of them all summer long except at the fair. We'd shriek, as young girls will do, when we spotted each other and then, sharing weeks of pent-up secrets, we'd make endless trips up and down the gaudy midway. It was filled with rows and rows of incandescent light bulbs, with carousel music—and with wicked con artists! My parents advised me to invest my allowance in pink cotton candy and not at the dishonest booths. But I loved hearing the greasy-looking scalawags yell at me to come throw the ball, and sometimes I wasted a quarter in spite of my parents' warnings.

Flirting was a championship event at the county fair, of course. One year, when we were about fourteen, my cousin Judy and I spent an entire day working on our joint entry. We twigged our hair and evaluated every outfit in our closets for potential glamour. We thought we'd never looked better and would surely turn some heads. I have to smile looking at the proud snapshot we asked Daddy to take of us minutes before we left for the fair.

Judy, in her full skirt and crinolines and puffy hair, looks like a balloon ready to take sail. I, with my razor short do frizzled on top, my long neck, and limp, polka dot dress, look for all the world like a giraffe wearing Tangee orange lip gloss. But we felt pretty, and I guess that is what matters.

Back then, Martha Stewart had not yet made a zillion dollars out of branding "homemade." All of us girls were just expected to be able to cook and sew, and the 4-H Club helped our mothers teach us. We were required to have an entry at the fair in either sewing or foods to complete our 4-H project and get a pin (or certificate or something.) I quickly flunked sewing as I didn't have the patience to even thread a needle, so punted to "foods" for my 4-H glory. I easily won blue ribbons the years we were required to enter cookies, then brownies, then fudge. My nadir was the angel food cake year.

My first two efforts at baking fair worthy food for angels morphed into shortbread and didn't rise at all. The third attempt was as lopsided as an angel's sliding board. Finally, at midnight before opening day of the fair, I whipped up a Duncan Hines cake mix in desperation. Oddly, this was not against the 4-H Club rules for project completion, but I felt like a cheat. That was the beginning of my life of crime as a counterfeit cook, I realize now, but it wasn't such a bad lesson for a girl to learn. There are more important things in a woman's life than making cakes (regardless of what Martha Stewart says!)

In my late teens, the county fair meant summertime dates with tanned young men at the Saturday night horse show. The very words "Tennessee Walking Horse" are synonymous to me with English Leather aftershave lotion and Mrs. Tandy's syncopated electric organ music.

I also had my fifteen seconds of fame about that time. I'd dumped the Tangee, shed the skinny giraffe look, and let my hair grow a little longer. For one enchanted night I glimpsed the world of Miss America when I was crowned with rhinestones as Miss Owen County Fair. (That was in 1961 in case any readers are counting on their fingers.)

Thirteen years later, I took our oldest daughter to the county fair. She was two that summer, and her grandparents and I were looking forward to introducing the merry-go-round to another generation. Shan's enthusiasm did not disappoint us. We each took turns riding with her until we were so dizzy we could barely stand. When my father pulled her from the wooden horse hours later, Shan cried and cried and cried. "Hortie," she said, "Hortie." I can still hear the catch in Daddy's voice when he said he'd never had to make her cry before.

Earlier this spring, I tried to introduce our three-year-old grandson, Owen, to the merry-go-round. It was about the grandest one I'd ever seen and was plopped down just north of the life-size dinosaur exhibit and across from the rain forest in the magnificent, world-class Indianapolis Children's Museum. Well, the merry-go-round terrified Owen, and I ended up riding alone. I waved to him as I climbed onto a colorful steed, and he bravely smiled and waved back at me. Maybe next time, we agreed.

And maybe, I realized, painted wooden ponies can only race as high as the sky on humid July nights after feeding on pink cotton candy. Maybe they drink English Leather aftershave and dance only to Mrs. Tandy's electric organ music. Maybe the county fair is their natural habitat.

Our First Vacation

In August of 1956, Daddy observed that his tobacco crop needed another couple of weeks to yellow in the fields before cutting. If my mother and I wanted, he allowed as how he could slip away from the farm work for a few days, and we could join his sisters and their families on a short vacation trip to the Smokey Mountains.

Did we want to? I was eleven years old and I'd wanted to "SEE ROCK CITY" ever since I'd learned to read the signs plastered on every barn between home and Lexington. We'd never taken a vacation before unless you counted the dash we'd made to Illinois for Uncle Henry's funeral. That trip hadn't been a barrel of laughs, but still, I'd enjoyed seeing the Midwest's flat as a pancake land for the first time in my life. Now we'd go the other direction, and I'd get to see real mountains.

The beauty of a road trip with a vague destination is that you can enjoy all the stops along the way. And when you've never been anywhere, everything is worth seeing. We stopped at the pullover as we approached the Kentucky River palisades and marveled at this wonder so near our home. We gawked at the gaudy bedspreads hung out for sale on the side of the road though we decided we wouldn't have one if you gave it to us. We bought sticky candy at Stuckey's. We pulled off U.S. 25 at Dogpatch short of the Tennessee line and toured the small zoo. That's where the monkey reached out of his cage and pulled my hair. I didn't blame him. I'd be mad too if I'd ended up in a smelly cage at tacky Dogpatch, but still, I've never liked monkeys much since then.

And then we reached the Smokey Mountains, taller and grander than I'd even dared imagine. What I loved most, though,

159

was the traveling, the hot wind rushing in the open car windows as we dashed along the curvy, two lane highways at a reckless 50 miles an hour. My cousin Judy and I—she was the same age as me—would scan the billboards to select our night's lodging. Motels were the latest, greatest thing in 1956. No antiquated hotels in small towns for us! We wanted to stay where we could pull our car right up to our bedroom door. We demanded air-conditioning though neither of us had that luxury at home. And sliding, glass shower doors were a must. Judy and I played elevator half one night with those.

Eating all our meals in restaurants was fun too. I'd never seen crinkle cut French fries before, but the most exotic item was the jelly served each morning at breakfast in tiny plastic sealed containers. The waitresses were generous with the jellies—and so Judy and I squirreled away the extras for the day when our vacation would be only a sweet memory.

We collected jellies in different colors much the way beach-combers search for variety in shells. For safety's sake, we stashed our treasures on the wide back shelf under the rear window of Uncle Melvin's Buick. When we got tired of watching for Burma Shave jingles spiked in couplets on the highway's shoulder, we'd pull our jellies down, and count and sort them by flavor.

It was ninety-five degrees in the back seat and we were thirty minutes south of lunch somewhere in east Tennessee when Aunt Neb screamed.

"What's wrong?" Uncle Melvin asked. There was concern in his voice.

"I don't have my teeth," Aunt Neb managed to get out. She'd gotten false teeth a week before we'd left on our trip, and they'd put a crimp in her vacation fun. She was forever taking them out doing this and that with them. "I bet I left them back at that restaurant," she sobbed.

Uncle Melvin slammed on the brakes and the Buick came to an abrupt stop on the side of the highway. "You've lost your teeth?" His voice was incredulous. "You've lost your teeth," he said again. His voice was getting irritated now.

On Lookout Mountain: l-r, Uncle Melvin Phillips, Aunt Neb & Cousin Pam; Cousin Judy & Uncle Louis Lowrance; Uncle Melvin's dad, George; and Georgia, her father and her mother.

The other car in our caravan screeched to a halt behind us. Like town criers, Judy and I shouted out our window in its direction, "AUNT NEB'S LOST HER TEETH."

Before he'd backtrack to the restaurant, Uncle Melvin declared that the entire car would be emptied and searched. Surely, the missing teeth were in the car. So out we all climbed. We stood silent in the weeds, in blue cornflowers and Queen Anne's lace, while Uncle Melvin pushed his hands into every crevice of the car's seats. Then, his face red with heat and disgust, his arm swept the rear shelf under the back window. He cleared it of everything in hopes the missing teeth would pop out of hiding.

All that popped however were our thirty-five boxes of melted jellies. They went flying upward toward Tennessee skies, and apricot, grape and strawberry rained down on the windshields of passing truckers.

161

Judy started to cry, "Our jellies—" but I shushed her. I sensed it was not the moment to assert property rights. And then, oh then, I swear it's true—

Aunt Neb whispered, "I've found my teeth."

We went on lots of other family trips after that. In time, I traveled to the other side of the world and back. But I've never topped those magic jelly days, so sweet and easy you could forget false teeth were resting in your mouth.

Grass Chiggers and Blackberries

I used to think that grass chiggers stalked everyone's childhood, but to my amazement, I've run into people from other parts of the country who don't know about them. By rights, the chigger should be our official state insect—if we must have one. After all, the epicenter of the parasite's international breeding grounds lies in Kentucky, possibly on our Owen County farm. But no, Kentucky bestows that dubious honor to the viceroy butterfly, an elegant bug, I admit, but why should personality and good looks dominate every election?

The chigger does keep good company, though. The blackberry, its best friend, is Kentucky's official fruit—which is the exception that breaks the rule. Classy breeding and a moneyed background don't always win out in these contests. The blackberry is a weed with thorns, effortlessly fertile when married to our limestone soil. Since Ernie and I have now given up even the pretense of farming, its unruly brambles are running wild on our place.

I got to thinking about this relationship between larvae and fruit this week when I had a passing notion to pluck some organic, mine-but-for-the-getting blackberries on our farm. In July, the fleshy berries come of age in Owen County. They outgrow their adolescent blushing and mature into Rubenesque black beauties. Like the Sirens who lured sailors into shipwreck with songs of desire, the succulent berries seduce the greedy and the innocent alike to wade into the briar patch.

Then I remembered. The summer I was four Mother and I went on a serious blackberry expedition on the overgrown hillside beyond the far pond. Miz Zell True, one of my favorite grown-ups, joined us. She told good stories and made everything fun, so I was excited about our adventure.

Miz Zell told me how we would sprinkle the berries like sunshine on cereal in the morning, and splash milk and sugar over them for an afternoon treat and invite the Gingerbread Man to join us. She told me about the sugary cobbler Mother would make for our supper, and described how we'd preserve jars of thick jam to spread on hot biscuits to remind us of the taste of summer when winter came.

In their defense, the women dressed me appropriately for berry picking in long pants and sleeves. Maybe I got hot and pulled the protective clothing up or down or off. I do recall that I took along my doll, a boy named Johnny, and kept dropping him in the grass that grows undisturbed beneath the berry briers.

By the end of the day, I'd lost Johnny for good, to everyone's dismay. But I brought home hundreds, maybe even a thousand, chigger bites. Mother couldn't put the head of a straight pin between the itching red welts that stretched from my scalp to the innards of my toes.

For those who haven't been terrorized by the parasitic red bug, I guess I should explain how they operate. They're somewhat more complex than I realized when I was a kid. The University of Kentucky's College of Agriculture website has this to say:

> Chiggers overwinter as adults in the soil, becoming active in the spring. Eggs are laid on the soil. After hatching, the larvae crawl about until they locate and attach to a suitable host. The larvae do NOT burrow into the skin, but inject a salivary fluid which produces a hardened, raised area around them. Body fluids from the host are withdrawn through a feeding tube. Larvae feed for about 4 days and then drop off and molt to nonparasitic nymphs and adults. Chiggers feed on a variety of wild and domestic animals, as well as humans.

I would add that chigger larvae thrive in the vegetation that grows unmown beneath the prickly blackberry canes. And when given the chance, they prefer to feed on humans, especially the tender skin in one's most private places. As a fair skinned four year old, however, I was delectable from end to end.

We'd never heard of anti-itching medicines like Benadryl. I don't think we even had calamine lotion. But we did have coal oil, my grandfather's cure for everything. I'm not sure what that is since the phrase has vanished from the lexicon, but I think it's kerosene. Whatever it is, it was Gran's elixir, and he proceeded to fill a galvanized washtub with coal oil and cold water.

I was too miserable to resist when he dunked me under. In my memory, the itching did subside some then, but the burning began. I was in agony for days until my welts broke open, oozed, and eventually scabbed over. The rest of my childhood was not chigger-bite-free, of course, but the larvae never again got a chance to mutilate my body because—being no fool—I avoided the blackberry patch, its primary lair, like the plague.

And so I decided not to go blackberry picking at the farm last week. Instead, I purchased some fine berries—on sale, too—at the supermarket. They probably emigrated from Ecuador while local blackberries go begging, but there is a limit to how politically correct I can stand to be.

The Dog Days of August

The Dog Days of August are upon us although I'm not sure when they begin or end. All I know is that the thermometer hit a hundred in my part of Kentucky this week, and the dogs, too hot to trot, all lay down and took a long nap to keep from going mad. There was a time when dogs sought out the shade of the closest tree for their August siestas. Now, like the rest of us, they hide out in air-conditioned buildings when the temperature goes above ninety.

In the millennium of my childhood—before dinosaurs, before the invention of the wheel, before electrically cooled air—people, like dogs, sought relief from the August heat in shady spots out-of-doors. We escaped to the outside especially at nighttime when our upstairs bedrooms morphed into the fiery furnaces of hell.

My family would adjourn to the wide front porch of our white clapboard farmhouse, and postpone bedtime until it cooled off enough to sleep a little. Even a kid—if she was smart enough to keep quiet—was allowed to stay up as long as it took for the temperature to become bearable inside.

The humid smell of August, sweet with some unidentified flower, would settle into our nostrils, and we would sit there barely moving while twilight faded into pitch dark. We'd sip ice tea and fan ourselves with a folded sheet of the *Lexington Herald*. Listening to the sex crazed frenzy of the crickets and tree frogs, we'd sigh, mop perspiration from our foreheads with the back of our hand, and count the lightning bugs flying higher and higher until it was hard to tell them from the Dog Star, itself.

When the mix of heat and night and sound and smells was exactly right, the grown-ups would begin to tell stories about people they had known. Sometimes the stories were funny, sometimes sad. But they always had a point, some small lesson about the hardships or joys of life, about relationships, or the handling of work and business that should not be forgotten by the storyteller or the listener.

Someone would conclude these accounts with an old saying like, "You know what they say—" Shirtsleeves to shirtsleeves in three generations, for example, was a reflection on the difficulty of hanging on to inherited money. Pride goeth before a fall, pretty is as pretty does, haste makes waste. Listening in the dark, my sense of right and wrong, of oughts and ambitions, took shape.

I had a jolt of recognition when I ran across journalist Russell Baker's best-selling autobiography *Growing Up.* His childhood summer nights with his West Virginia relatives were much like mine in Owen County, Kentucky. Baker made the assertion that everything of value that he had learned in life could be summarized in those old bromides he overheard on the nighttime porches of his youth.

I was so taken with this notion that I decided to ask my own adult children if they'd been impacted in a similar way by old sayings I'd shared with them. I did this despite knowing full well that I'd brought them up in an air conditioned suburb, and that they'd rarely seen a front porch, much less sat on one and sipped sweet tea in the dark. I don't know why I was surprised when they looked at me as though I'd lost my mind.

After a long silence, one of them ventured, "Go with the flow?"

Now any mother who's ever stuffed three children into the back seat of a sedan for a long car trip, will understand why I repeated that advice so often to my girls over the years. Still, I'd hoped something a little more profound might have stuck with them. After all, I hadn't set out to raise wimpy conformists. I only wanted to get from point A to point B without having to pull over to the shoulder of the highway and shoot one of them. But the thing about going with the flow is that it's best understood—and most appreciated—in its absence.

167

Take the story, for example, that my son-in-law Tim likes to tell about the family trip he and his three siblings and his parents once took. As noon approached, his dad asked where the kids would like to stop for a quick lunch. Everyone agreed on Long John Silver's seafood restaurant—except for his little sister who insisted on going to McDonald's. She pitched such a fit that she prevailed over the objections of her brothers, and persuaded her father to pull in at the golden arches. When it came time to place their orders—you guessed it—she asked for a fish sandwich.

Perhaps going with the flow is a pretty good life lesson to pass on to my children after all. Maybe they won't get caught up Cripple Creek without a paddle. Maybe going with the flow is the only way to survive the Dog Days of August.

Halloween Failures

I once knew a man who got kicked out of his Blue Christmas therapy group because he was a little bit too cheerful. I thought about him last week as I stumbled through yet another Halloween.

For some, Halloween is all about the supernatural, the scary stuff like the living dead and werewolves. NPR reports that community haunted houses will take in revenue approaching a million dollars this month, and here in Kentucky, a Danville woman got so frightened touring the Jaycee Haunted House, she jumped out the second story window and broke both her legs. For others the October holiday is over the top fun, mammoth Styrofoam spiders climbing up suburban chimneys, giant Casper the Friendly Ghost balloons tied to the lamppost, and strings of pumpkin lights draped over every shrub in sight.

Between the two extremes there's little room for the likes of me who can only muster a little bit of cheerful. Truth is, I'm mediocre at Halloween, maybe a failure. When I carve Jack O Lanterns they turn out more like exhibit A for a malpractice suit than either cute or menacing. And they go squishy before All Hallows Eve.

Then there's the Trick or Treat candy. I start out with discipline and on the cheap. I scan the sale bin for sacks of mixed anonymous lumps that no one, even I, could lust for. But at the appointed hour, as the raven quotes "Nevermore," I start to worry that our loot won't measure up to what the neighbors are giving away. And what if we should run out—though of course we never have. I dash to Kroger on my broomstick, and grab a few bushels of super-sized, over-priced bags of Reese's Cups and Snickers Bars and gain my annual Halloween five pounds.

169

As if chocolate and Jack O Lanterns are not challenging enough for me, I was born without the creative costume gene. Despite a college degree in theater, I'm untalented at coming up with "going to be at Halloween" ideas. The best I ever did was the year I sent Becky out dressed in cardboard as a Cheerios box. Then, last week, my favorite comic strip character was ridiculed off the funny page when she went Trick or Treating as her favorite breakfast cereal. Sigh.

You have to understand that my girls' elementary school was the Paris, France, of Halloween costumes. The children's annual parade through the streets of our little town, Russell, garnered as much attention as the unveiling of a *haute couture* collection. The police blocked traffic. The mayor showed up with the editor of the newspaper. The townspeople lined the sidewalks to root for their favorites. It was Project Runway before cable existed.

This competitiveness caught me by surprise when my oldest daughter entered school. As a kid growing up at Natlee, I'd been delighted by thrown-together-from-out-of-the-rag-bag hoboes and ghosts. So I thought I'd outdone myself when I discovered ready-made plastic outfits at Kmart. I plucked a cartoon character off the rack, and draped it on her.

How was I to know that all the other moms had spent the previous twelve months crafting heirloom creations? The Tin Man and the Cowardly Lion who looked like they'd just said good-bye to the Wizard and walked off the movie set. A museum quality Raggedy Ann with every strand of red yarn hair hand-looped and hand-knotted. A Cookie Monster with real fur dyed blue and giant eyes that moved. Oh, the list goes on and on. It was enough to make a grown woman weep, and I did. My only consolation over the years we endured these parades was that my children didn't seem to notice how tacky they looked in their plastic, off the rack embarrassments.

Now, as I watch them ready our grandchildren for Hallow-een, I grasp how much I damaged their self-esteem with my discount store ensembles. With military precision, they plan and discuss their costume options for a year in advance, and the kids go out to beg for candy in get-ups more expensive than a winter coat. Maybe two winter coats. This year, a national run on Mario

Brothers outfits created a family crisis. Eliza's "Peach" and Owen's "Toad the Mushroom" arrived on schedule, but Jared's "Luigi" suit was backordered. For a frantic month, Becky wrung her hands fearing it wouldn't arrive in time.

Trying to be cheerful, I suggested our grandson might find a suitable substitution in plastic down at the Kmart. Becky gave me the "Oh, Mother" look, and returned to her Internet search for the last Luigi costume in America. She succeeded, and with a "HA" in her voice informed me that all the effort was worth it. Jared was such a standout at his Halloween outings, he said he felt like one of the Jonas Brothers.

I wonder if I could locate that guy who got kicked out of his Blue Christmas therapy group? Maybe he'd like to come over and watch "It's a Wonderful Life" with me for the next two months and help me eat all these leftover Reese's Cups.

The Thanksgiving Blizzard of 1950

Our three adult daughters, their husbands, and our grand-children will gather at our house on Thanksgiving Day. Anyone with much family will understand what a feat it is—and what a joy—to have everybody home together at anytime, but especially for a holiday.

I want to make the day perfect, something our grandchildren will remember for the rest of their lives. Even the youngest of them, I hope, will internalize the spirit of the day, if not the details.

But even as I make my preparations, I know that it is often disaster, rather than perfection, that makes a holiday hang in memory. The assassination of John F. Kennedy dominates the only Thanksgiving I remember clearly from my young adult years. More recently, I think of my Mother's final Thanksgiving as she lay in a hospital bed measuring out the last thirty days of her life.

And from the millennium of my childhood, I only remember one. The Thanksgiving of 1950.

When I was growing up, Thanksgiving was a low-key holi-day for my family. My father, and several of his siblings, were tobacco farmers, and Thanksgiving week was a prime time to strip tobacco. The annual market opened the next week, and Daddy liked to have part of the crop on the first auction when prices were usually highest.

But in 1950, Daddy's city brothers organized a Thanksgiv-ing Day dinner at Mawmaw and Pawpaw Green's place. It's the only time I recall the large, Green clan celebrating Thanksgiving together, and Daddy felt obliged to go. Old Mr. Hammond, who was working for Daddy, and my maternal grandfather, Gran Hudson, volunteered to stay behind and strip tobacco.

It was a clear day when my parents and I set out on the thirty-mile trip to my grandparents' farmhouse at the top of the Sparta hill. I don't remember much else about the day. I presume it was like our many Christmas gatherings, events I recall with more clarity. There would have been a potluck feast, with turkey taking second place to old country ham. There would have been macaroni and cheese casseroles with crackers crumbled on top, Jello salads, sweet potatoes, and blackberry jam cake. The men would have played loud games of Rook all day at card tables set up in the front parlor. The children would have found cubbies where they could play in the over-crowded house, on the steps or even in the bathroom when it was available.

But sometime in the afternoon, it began to snow. At first, everyone was casual about the flurries that were coming fast and steady. Before anyone realized what was happening, the roads were covered.

My grandparents and the aunts and uncles urged us not to hurry away. There was plenty of food, they said, and the roads probably would be better later when the snow stopped. If they weren't, well then, we could spend the night on one of the feather beds piled under the sloped ceiling attic bedrooms under the eaves. But Daddy, worried about the tobacco and the farm animals, decided we had to get home. Slipping and sliding, we scooted along the rollercoaster highway from Sparta to Owenton. I was scared to death because I could tell Daddy was. He stopped in Owenton, roughly the halfway point of our journey, and bought the last set of tire chains at the Texaco Station.

By now the snow, mixed with sleet, was getting deep and starting to drift. We had seventeen miles left to travel on the crookedest roads in the county. It took us two hours, but with the help of God and the tire chains, we plowed the curves home in the dark. The car wouldn't budge again for the next five days.

The men tunneled a passage through the drifts to the barn-yard and the tobacco stripping room, and the work went on. Mr. Hammond, of course, could not go home. He was a huge man who enjoyed eating, and having been a widower for years, he was delighted to be snowed in with Mother's home cooking. I can still see him laughing beneath his huge handlebar mustache as he heaped another helping onto his plate.

In a few days, though, Mother ran out of food, even flour and coffee. Daddy saddled up our workhorse, Old Nell, to ride to the country store at Natlee. I stood at the front window and watched him vanish into the white landscape. Later, when I read Wilder's Little House books about winters on the prairie, all I could picture was Old Nell sinking into the drifts up to her haunches and Daddy clinging to her neck.

Most of the things I remember from my childhood are smaller, diminished, when I re-visit them as an adult. But the Thanksgiving blizzard of 1950 is counted among the worst, maybe the worst, to ever strike the eastern United States. Meteorologists study its mathematical model to predict such catastrophes even today. The storm impacted 22 states, killed 383 people, and created estimated damages of $70 million in 1950 dollars. It dumped up to fifty-seven inches of snow in some areas. Winds reached forty miles an hour. Twenty-five foot drifts piled up and froze in sub-zero temperatures. One million customers lost power. And Michigan played Ohio State in a whiteout, advancing to the Rose Bowl without achieving even one first down.

In time, the snow vanished, and old Mr. Hammond went home to his canned pork'n beans and bologna. Our city relatives, who'd been stranded at Mawmaw and Pawpaw Green's small farmhouse for days, went home too. The tobacco went to market, and the normal rhythm of our lives resumed.

Aunt Neb

Today there is one less person in the world who loves me. Aunt Neb, the last of Daddy's siblings, died this morning. Though she was closing in on her 91st birthday, her death caught me by surprise. She was clear of mind. She walked without a cane and drove herself to the grocery and to church. Until a week ago, she lived alone in the house her late husband built for her in 1955, the one with steps leading up to the front door and down to the basement garage. Last Monday, she finally gave in to her family's pleading, and moved into an apartment in a senior housing development to pacify them, or as she phrased it, to shut them up.

My cousin Judy and I visited with her and her daughter yesterday afternoon, and Aunt Neb peppered us with questions as she always did about the lives and limbs of our respective families. I showed her pictures of my newest grandchild. She described the cake that would be served at her granddaughter's upcoming wedding, her gift to the young couple. She also wiggled her bare feet for us. She was proud that they had no bunions, corns, or crooked toes. I confess that I was a tad envious of them and her trim, unswollen ankles, too.

But the truth is—death always takes me by surprise. I am not genetically engineered to expect it even when doctors have told me that each breath could be my loved one's last. The people I love seem immortal to me, and I mean here on earth, not in heaven. I understand that this isn't rational, but I suspect that most folks, if honest, feel the same way. Other people have to die of course, other people's parents, aunts and uncles, spouses, siblings, and children. But our own? No.

And so I'm reeling in disbelief that my aunt—the repository of my family's memory and so alive yesterday—is gone today. I think of the cliché about never putting off until tomorrow, and I'm grateful that I made the seventy-mile trip from Lexington to Erlanger on a sunny Saturday afternoon to chat with her.

Santa Claus

I spotted Santa Claus sitting in a large easy chair as soon as I entered our church's back foyer. It doubles as a fellowship hall on Sundays between services, and it's a popular spot where talk flows along with the hot coffee.

Although he was disguised in a white shirt and tie and a khaki windbreaker, I knew who he was. His long white beard gave him away.

"Santa Claus!" I called out, making my way toward him through the crowd of Methodists wolfing down doughnuts. He was chatting with one of the homeless men who attend services at our downtown Lexington church. Interrupting them, I blurted out,

"Do you remember me? Georgia Stamper? We knew each other in Ashland when I lived there. How wonderful to run into you here!"

He has family in Lexington, he said, as he looked up at me with his blue eyes, a little milky now with age. Then he took my outstretched hand in both of his. I was startled that his felt so boney. Didn't he used to be fleshier?

"I brought my daughters to visit you every year at Hills Department Store. That would have been in the late 1970s. I never bothered taking them to any of those impostors from central casting. They only talked to you."

He smiled and nodded as though he did recall my little girls, mothers now themselves.

I burbled on as people will do with the very old so that Santa wouldn't have to talk if he didn't want to, if he were too tired, if he didn't remember me.

"My oldest grandson is in boy scouts, now, for almost a year, and it's been a life changing experience for him." Not many people know that Santa has been in scouting almost as long as it has existed. Once, on Scout Sunday back in Ashland, I heard him talk about meeting Lord Baden-Powell, the founder of the scouting movement, at one of the early World Scout Jamborees.

"That's fine news about your grandson," he said in a quiet voice. I believed he meant it, as if he were as concerned about the boy's well-being as I am.

Then, abruptly returning to our earlier subject, he said, "Those years at Hills were good ones. I'd just retired from forty years on the railroad and was looking for a way to be useful. I went to every store in Ashland and Russell, all the big places like Sears and J. C. Penney and Parsons, but the only one that would give me the time of day was Hills. One incident—I've never forgotten."

He paused and stroked his beard as if considering how best to tell me this story. I wondered what could be so unusual that it would hang in Santa's memory for decades. Remembering the bizarre incidents in David Sedaris' "SantaLand Diaries," I prepared myself for something funny.

"A little girl came to see me one day. She could have been as old as nine, a tall child on the chunky side, but I suspect she was large for her age because she had the manner of a child about six." Santa shuffled the cane propped against his knee and looked away from me as though he were clarifying her image in his mind. After a few moments he looked back at me and went on.

"One half of her face was the most beautiful chocolate color I've ever seen. The rich brown color ran on a diagonal line from her upper left hairline, across her nose, and ended on her lower right jaw line." Santa sliced his face into two imaginary triangles with his hand so that I would understand.

"But the opposite half of her face, following the same diagonal slant, was splotched with many colors, white, purple, blue, and it was bumpy with growths." In a quiet way, Santa also swept his hand over this triangle of his face to help me visualize what he had seen.

178

"We chatted a few minutes about what she wanted for Christmas. And then, as I did for every child who came to talk with me, I kissed her on the cheek and gave her a peppermint candy cane. Then I lifted her off my lap, and she took off running.

"I was stationed in the rear of the store in a wide center aisle that allowed me to see all the way to the front entrance. And so I could see her running down that long aisle, nearly the length of a football field, to where her family stood near the front of the store, and I could hear her shouting to them as she ran—'Santa Claus kissed me on the cheek! He kissed me on the cheek!' she yelled out to them, over and over and over."

Santa stopped speaking, and stared at something I could not see. We sat in silence as others bustled past us, in a hurry now to finish their coffee and settle themselves in the large sanctuary of our church for the eleven o'clock service. Minutes passed. I reached for his hand and squeezed it gently to say good-bye. The old man acknowledged my leaving with only the slightest nod of his head.

I confess that I didn't hear the choir sing that morning or anything the minister said. I sat in my padded pew thinking about the little girl with the Joker face and wondering who she might be now, over thirty years later.

This then is my message to you, gentle reader, by way of Santa Claus and with words borrowed from the poet Emily Dickinson:

If I can stop one heart from breaking, I shall not live in vain.

The Ghosts of Christmas Past

It was the week after Christmas, not the night before, and I was the mother of grown children, not a child. Still, I lay awake in the second floor bedroom of my childhood home listening to the noises an old house will make in the dark. My father had died earlier in the day. Yet I heard his hand on the back porch door, his footstep on the basement stairs, his movement in the kitchen. Rain gusted against the dormer windows and sleep would not come. Ghosts live only in stories I told myself.

The wind blows in cities. But the close buildings divert it, tunneling it down one-way streets and dead-end alleys with scraps of trash and the occasional hat. A careful man like Norman could escape the slap of a north wind's hand and ignore most of its noise in a tight Cincinnati apartment.

In Kentucky, though, on an Owen County farm, when your house sits on a high hill, the wind comes right on in and joins you at the supper table. And so on that long ago Christmas Eve when the familiar wailing began to blare from the second floor bedrooms where I'd slept most every night of my life, none of us gave it a second thought. Except for Norman.

"What's that?" he asked. The question startled me coming as it did in the middle of his slide presentation—a documentary of the graves of all U. S. presidents up through FDR. Norman was a man who traveled. Once he'd even gone to Europe and brought me back a blue nylon scarf. But mostly he visited the tombs of presidents.

"Is this house haunted?" he asked. He spoke in a fast, staccato rhythm that I took to be an educated midwestern accent since he'd studied at the Cincinnati Conservatory of Music. At first I thought he was kidding, but then he asked again, "Dexter, have you heard ghosts before?" The look on his face told me he was not joking. His thumbs fidgeted with his leather suspenders as he waited for my father to answer.

Now Daddy was the only farmer I ever knew who used algebra in real life to figure up things like how much hayseed he needed to buy for the back pasture. Suffice it to say, he didn't believe in ghosts. But ever kind, he hesitated, considering how to answer his guest. Great-Uncle Murphy jumped in to rescue him.

"Ghosts?" Uncle Murphy asked. His voice cradled the grin spreading across his face. He crossed one thin leg over the other and ran a boney hand through his still-red hair. "You mean like haints?" and then he chuckled.

Uncle Murphy had been gassed on the battlefields of Europe in World War I, and the Army had sent him home to die on a military disability pension. A stubborn man, he decided to refuse death's invitation. Instead, he went back to work on his Kentucky farm and would work every day for the rest of his life until he toppled over at the age of ninety-seven. On this Christmas Eve, he had about thirty more years of labor ahead of him. He wasn't the sort of man who took stock in ghosts.

Then Aunt Bessie chimed in. "Ghosts! Norman, all that education has touched you in the head."

She finished up with her signature "aw–ee" that was a cross between a pig farmer calling shoats and an Irish washerwoman keening at her first-born's wake. She punctuated all her conversations with aw–ee to emphasize whatever point she might be making. In this case her point was that she didn't hold with anything Uncle Murphy didn't believe in.

"aaAW—EE" she let loose, soaring to her highest register. More than once she had made Mother's crystal ring at the table. Though showing her age by the time I can remember her, Aunt Bessie was still a pretty pudding of a woman, soft and round and rouged. Perhaps that was why her aw–ee was considered charming as opposed to alarming.

Right on cue, the upstairs windows answered her. "WWOOoooWWOOooo—"

Norman began gathering his slides and shoving them back into the slotted carrier. He did this without looking, and I

181

wondered if that explained why it always took him four attempts to get a slide positioned right side up in his manual projector.

"I need to be off now. It's getting late—"

Mother interrupted him. "Oh, Norman—don't go—we haven't cut the jam cake yet." I understood that Mother was changing the subject to help Norman save face. A high school science teacher, she was a non-ghost-believer for certain, but she would never embarrass anyone.

All the aunts and uncles and cousins were smiling now, but I was choking on giggles. I was going on thirteen and considered myself an intellectual. I had, after all, plodded through Daddy's bookshelf of classic novels when I had the flu the winter before. A girl who'd read Henry Fielding sure didn't believe in ghosts.

In fact, nobody in my family believed in ghosts. Except now, apparently, for Norman though he technically wasn't a relative but a cousin of cousins. A bachelor with no siblings, Norman became a regular at our holiday tables when he found himself orphaned in middle age.

For his part, Norman brought a bit of the exotic to our parties. He was a Republican—a capitalist, he called himself, living on income from an inheritance—thrown into a lions' den of working class FDR Democrats. He defended his political positions with passion in the debates that dominated our family get-togethers. He was also a non-pork eating Seventh Day Adventist set adrift in a sea of Methodists who worshiped old country ham.

I thought he had the look of a senator though I'd never seen one in the flesh. He was distinguished in the way a statesman should be, always wearing a tie and his navy serge suit with his dark, thinning hair combed straight back. Let's put it this way. He was good enough looking that Aunt Bessie never gave up hope that he would marry. And from time to time, he would bring a lady friend to dinner. The romances never lasted long—but they encouraged Aunt Bessie and gave her conversational fodder for decades at a stretch.

"Norman, don't go. Let me tell you about the windows," Daddy said.

"We built this house on the cheap in '49 when the old one burned. You know how it was after the war—everybody gone off to work in factories—and I don't know if the contractor was ignorant or trying to save a dime, but those jackleg carpenters hung the dormer windows wrong and the seals never closed right. Whenever the wind comes certain ways, the windows set in making that noise. "

Then he said, "Come on, walk upstairs with me, I'll show you what I'm talking about."

To prove to Norman that our house was not haunted, I jumped up and offered to go with them. If a thirteen-year-old girl wasn't scared of the noises our windows made, surely Norman would be convinced.

I started up the stairs first to make the point. Put on the spot like that, Norman followed, and Daddy brought up the rear. As we made our way up the narrow stairs, the windows let loose with an orchestration of woo-hoos that made the 1812 Overture sound like a lullaby. Even I began to feel nervous. Norman turned white. But Daddy, blocking our escape route, wouldn't let us turn around.

When we reached the dormer room, Daddy flipped on all the lights, then he insisted that Norman and I stand next to the windows. "Woo-woo," the windows screamed, over and over, until goose bumps were standing on my skin.

But none of us saw any ghosts. None of us felt any ghosts either. When beads of perspiration began to run down Norman's face, Daddy took pity, and suggested we go back downstairs and have jam cake with the others.

Decades later, hours after my father's death, I lay awake in a second floor bedroom of my childhood home. The wind blew, and once again I heard the old windows talking. I thought of Norman and Daddy and all the other ghosts of Christmases past, and smiled. Sweet sleep, sweet peace, came at last.

Butter in the Morning

prologue iv …

butter in the morning

A t twilight, two frogs were hopping through the barn when, by accident, they jumped off an edge into the farmer's half-full can of cream. Now an old-fashioned metal cream-can stands tall, about three feet off the floor, and it's only about 20 inches across. To the frogs, the cold, dark interior of the skinny can was a bewildering place. The first frog thought they might have landed in a hole on the ocean's floor. Or maybe they'd fallen off the edge of the earth. Perhaps they were even on the moon.

"Well, wherever we are, we'd better start paddling or we're going to drown," the second frog snapped, and so they did.

After a while, the first frog grew tired and discouraged.

"It's no use," he said. "We'll never get out of this hole." He quit paddling, went under, and drowned.

The second frog, however, kept paddling through the long night. When the sun rose in the morning, he found himself sitting high and dry on a fat pat of butter.

Mother shared this old story whenever anyone needed what she called "a pep talk." I've heard her tell it hundreds of times, and I think it is a fitting epitaph for her life. Certainly, she paddled hard until the end. She infused our home—and me—with this philosophy, but looking back I think that she, in turn, had absorbed it from our place. The people there, then, seldom quit. There are those who would point out that perseverance does not triumph in all situations. My mother and her kind were practical people and understood this. But yet, like the second frog, they saw no future in giving up. "Don't whine," they'd say, "paddle."

Georgia's Mother at Georgetown College. Circa 1941.

Mother

My daughter asks if she can donate my mother's old dresser to Goodwill. Close to fifteen years ago, we'd pulled it out of storage at the farmhouse for her first apartment, but after multiple moves, its finish is bruised and its drawers no longer glide. It looks out of place in her new suburban house with the granite countertops.

"No," I say, too quickly, without the appropriate hesitation, closing the discussion before it can begin, and so I add, "It's hard-rock maple. They don't make furniture that solid anymore." I ramble on about finding room for it at my house, though she and I know my place is over-stuffed. I'll have the drawers repaired, and maybe I'll even have it re-finished because, you know, it's hard-rock maple.

I refrain from telling her the back-story one more time because I know she knows it. How my parents bought the matching bedroom suite at Sears when we were homeless, a few days after the old house burned to the ground. The plain little dresser with its matching wooden handles stood in a corner of the downstairs bedroom for decades until it was replaced by a gleaming new cherry piece that caught Mother's eye. It was relegated, then, to an upstairs room, and finally left behind when Mother moved to an apartment after Daddy's death.

What I can't tell her, what I'm only beginning to understand myself, is that I'm afraid if I give away the dresser, I may lose my mother's face, the one not captured in photographs, the one I see in dim early memories as I stand off to the side watching her hands move over the dresser's smooth surface top, fingering her small arsenal of cosmetics to create the face she put on every

189

morning of her life to meet the world. How do I explain that to a grown-up daughter?

"I was never pretty," Mother would say matter-of-factly, as though she were commenting that the world was round and not flat. She had bright red hair, even as a newborn, Aunt Sis said. It wasn't strawberry blonde or auburn, but red, a notch, maybe two, darker than orange. Her eyebrows and her eyelashes were white, all their pigment re-directed into hundreds of freckles that covered her arms.

I am four, maybe five, and she is twenty-eight, maybe twenty-nine. I am watching her as she stares into the mirror that hangs above the dresser. She arches first one colorless eyebrow and then the other as she pencils them into life with Maybelline magic. Then, she swipes a doll-sized brush I covet, a tiny thing with a little handle, across a soft cake of mascara until the dark goo clings to the bristles. Holding her chin upward at a tilt and her head motionless, she looks toward the ceiling as she paints her invisible eyelashes brown.

Life can be harsh for women in hundreds of ways men find difficult to comprehend. Some shatter, or become bitter, or run away, or sink into depression, and I've glimpsed their shadows within myself. My mother, however, belonged to that tribe of females who can hold close the joy of living in spite of what life throws at them. They would describe themselves as ordinary, and would remind you that they are not rich or accomplished or acclaimed, that all they ever did was what needed to be done. They are not ordinary, of course, these modern amazons made of stuff more stable, more sturdy, than most of us. When I attempt to tell a little bit of my mother's story to others, however, I pull back. She begins to sound like an iron lady, someone I might be uncomfortable to be around, yet that wasn't the way she was at all. I remember her as the happiest of people, the kind who could make a drive down an unfamiliar country road seem as adventurous as a trip to Europe, the kind who never lost her childlike wonder at the beauty of Christmas lights or the color of a new tea rose. She was the softest of women, the kind who listen with compassion to the details of the school janitor's operation, the

190

kind who can coach a special ed student into a blue ribbon win at the science fair.

But I saw her cry for herself only twice. The first time was in that year after the house burned, when we had so little, and I, age four or five, knocked over the table by the chair and broke our only lamp. The second time, I was seventeen.

The doctor's appointment schedule had not allowed time for tact. "You have advanced glaucoma. A large chunk of your optic nerve in each eye has been destroyed, and you're going to go blind, maybe not tomorrow, but it's inevitable. All you can hope to do is delay it," the doctor said.

Mother was forty-one years old. She and I had made the trip to the Lexington ophthalmologist alone because Daddy was harvesting tobacco. A week earlier, we'd gone to the Kentucky State Fair where I'd competed in the 4-H Speech Contest. For a lark, we had wandered around the vast Exposition Hall signing up for prizes—I had my hopes pinned on a Florida vacation—and took advantage of every free sample, including health-screening tests. Mother had 20/20 vision and had never worn glasses even to read, but the technician working in the fair booth was alarmed at her elevated eye pressure. He advised her to see an ophthalmologist as soon as possible. Glaucoma, we learned, is a silent disease with almost no visual symptoms until you abruptly, and forever, lose sight.

She was explaining to me what the doctor had said, putting the best spin on it, but as we approached an intersection near our house, tears filled her eyes, and a quiet sob escaped her lips. Within moments, we hit the ditch on the side of the road. We weren't hurt. She righted the car.

Soon after that, she righted herself. That meant keeping track of twelve daily eye drops, sometimes fifteen when things weren't going well, administered on a rigid timetable for the next 44 years. Decade after decade, she set an alarm clock to wake herself for the middle-of-the-night dose. Sitting in a church pew before a granddaughter's wedding or at my aunt's funeral, anywhere, she would unobtrusively slip her bottle of eye drops from her purse. Holding her chin upward at a tilt and her head motionless, she would look towards the ceiling as though she were applying mascara, and without a sound, drop them in at the appointed hour.

She would instruct me to bully my way into surgery recovery rooms after her hip replacements, back operations, hernia repairs, to get her eye drops in on time. "We can't rely on the hospital staff to stick to the schedule, and my eye pressure will already be soaring because of the anesthesia," she'd say in her practical way. I'm not assertive by temperament, but I talked down arrogant surgeons to gain access to my mother, still half sedated, to lift her eyelids and drop in the medicine we prayed would keep her remaining thread of optic nerve intact. How could I have refused to do this when she wouldn't even take a pain pill because it might interfere with her glaucoma medicines? Not until the last week of her life did she let go of her regimen, but even then I don't think she had forgotten it. I believe she only stopped because life was over, and she gave herself permission, finally, to sleep without interruption.

When she died, two months shy of eighty-six, she could still read the morning newspaper. Her ophthalmologist—a younger, kinder doctor, Mother having long since outlived the first one or two—called me at home after her death, to grieve with me, to marvel at her discipline. He said she, not he, had saved her eyesight.

Mother was born in 1921 in her parents' four-room farmhouse. She was the second of two children, twelve years younger than Aunt Sis. By local measures, my grandparents were considered prosperous because they owned a good-sized farm that lay in the rich bottomland along the creek. Frugal people, they'd been out of debt when hard times hit, and were able to survive the Depression when others around them lost their farms. There was no cash money for anything beyond necessities, however, and their life was simple, even austere.

Mother would live out her life on the creek as generations of her family had done before her. She loved that land and its history, and would nurture it all her days on earth. She was a full working partner with my father on the farm, herding and vaccinating cattle, driving a tractor when he was shorthanded, and always, grooming and surveying the land, coaxing it, like herself, into doing its best. She would proudly introduce herself as a farmer to the end of her life.

Her girlhood ambition, however, was to become a doctor, maybe because she was smart and someone said she ought to aim high, maybe because my grandmother—as Mother herself would later be—was always sick with something. It was an implausible dream. Only about five percent of people entering medical school in that era were women, and her country high school didn't have a microscope or a semblance of a chemistry lab. Few of the local farm girls even went to college in the 1930s. Mother was undaunted. She graduated first in her small high school class, and set her sights on beginning her pre-med studies in the fall of 1939.

Only weeks after Mother's high school graduation, my forty-nine-year-old grandmother suffered a massive stroke. Aunt Sis was married and lived in a distant state. Nursing homes, if they existed, were for people abandoned by family, and there was little money to hire help to come in. The obvious solution was for Mother to postpone college to maintain the household and help nurse her mother. Whatever disappointment or resentment Mother may have felt was never shared with me. When she spoke of this time in her life, it was mostly always with laughter about her cooking and housekeeping mishaps.

It's difficult to explain to my daughters, who've never known a world without microwave ovens, how much labor it took to "keep house" on a farm in the 1930s. Even I, a generation closer to that time and place, am in awe of all that had to be done, day in and day out. All the food was prepared from scratch, and in my grandparents' home, cooking was done on a temperamental wood-burning stove. They thought their electric wringer washer was a great advancement over the washboards they'd used until a decade before, and it was. The water to fill it, however, had to be carried from a cistern a hundred yards from the house and then heated in a metal tub on top of the cook stove. After the laundry had been beaten clean by the machine's electric agitator, each piece was manually fed through the washer's wringer—which sometimes caught a finger too—and then hung outside to dry on a clothesline. In an era before no-wrinkle fabric existed, everything was starched and ironed.

My eighteen-year-old mother did all of this with only occasional help, including putting clean sheets on her mother's bed every day. When I questioned why she changed the bed linens daily, given the difficulty of laundering and ironing the sheets, she looked at me in surprise, as though the answer should be obvious. Finally, she said, "Because that's what you did when someone was bedridden."

I'm amazed she didn't drift into marriage with of one of the suitors who came around that year after high school. It would have been the easy thing to do. But in the fall of 1940, with my grandmother's health improved and with her blessing and encouragement, Mother packed her suitcase for college again, and boarded a Greyhound bus to pursue her dream of becoming a doctor.

She loved her time at Georgetown College. She met my father there in a chemistry class, joined a sorority, learned to dance, and made lifelong friends. Before she left, she'd also scored high enough on the MCAT examination to qualify for medical school.

Pearl Harbor, however, had shaken Mother's world. It seemed like the war would go on forever, she told me once. Money to go to medical school seemed impossible to find, she said. She had barely put together the money for college. She accepted a job teaching high school math and science a year and a half before she graduated, opting to go to summer school and interim terms to finish her degree. When Daddy came home on a furlough in August of 1943, they drove to Georgetown and were married in the living room of their college religion professor.

My grandmother had a second stroke in the summer of 1944, and this time she would not survive. With my grandfather left alone and grieving, and Daddy off in the war, Mother, now twenty-three, moved back to the farm to help. She continued teaching and saving money, but when I was born a few years later, she let go of her dream of becoming a doctor.

Perhaps it's just as well. She may have been too empathetic to endure the losses that are inevitable in medicine. Mother was all about hope and tomorrow, and that made her a fine teacher. Many of the farm kids she taught entered medical fields and related occupations such as engineering and research. On three occasions, her rural students advanced to the international level in science fair competition.

Georgia's Parents: Geraldine and Dexter Green.
Late fall, 1943.

I think Mother's gift, however, was her ability to encourage all types of students. She believed that you could do better, and for reasons I don't fully understand, you did. Maybe it was her enthusiasm, but I think it also had something to do with her faith in people. Letting her down didn't feel good.

Once, a woman I didn't know drove thirty miles to hear me speak. She wanted to absolve herself for an ill-conceived prank she'd instigated in Mother's class decades earlier. "She didn't punish us," the woman said, "but she looked so disappointed in us." I laughed, understanding.

Perhaps all children fear being orphaned, but I was aware early on that I could lose Mother, and that terrified me. I never went through a rebellious stage with her, in part because she was a sensitive and reasonable parent, but also because I had such a fear of her dying. She didn't dwell on her health problems, but it was obvious that she was sick more than other people's moms. From her early adulthood, she was plagued with myriad problems, the most severe being migraine headaches that flattened her for two days at a time, kidney disease that sent her to bed for six months, and high blood pressure, the villain that killed my grandmother. Arthritis, too, was always lurking around, slapping her to the ground at inconvenient times. Eventually, it would put her in a wheelchair the last decade of her life.

When I was a middle-aged woman and done with having babies, beyond being scared of my own body but experienced enough to understand, Mother began to talk more freely to me about the difficulties she'd had in childbirth. Having lost her mother early, she was determined to make her own family, surround herself with her own children. Yet each of her pregnancies brought complications that were life threatening. When she lost her last baby, her blood pressure soared to 300 over 200, and the doctor felt he could not safely give her an anesthesia. With Mother hemorrhaging and the infant already dead, they performed an emergency Caesarian with Novocaine injections.

Her darkest moment came when she drove home from the beauty shop one January day and saw my father and his tractor crashed at the bottom of the long, steep hill below the barn. Before she took a breath, before she tried to get to him, she called 911 and then neighbors for help. Hysteria was an indulgence Mother would not allow herself when doing was what was needed. The crying would come later when there was nothing more she could do for him.

Daddy was the center of Mother's life, and she never got over missing him. But she went on living, what else can you do, she said, with purpose and humor for another sixteen years. That span of time was important to our family. She helped me see my children grown, and me safely into late middle age. She remained at the helm of our family ship, sharing wisdom when asked, encouraging us through crisis, laughing and celebrating with us. A day came, though, when she said, "I have to turn the family over to you, now. I have my hands full with myself." I smiled, because I thought she wanted me to, as though she were making a joke, but I understood. It was her way of telling me how ill she had become.

When I look at photographs taken of Mother in her young adulthood, I agree that she wasn't pretty. She skipped over that adjective, and like the ugly duckling, grew up to be a swan. I know that I'm not objective though. I see Mother, not the picture. I am standing again beside the plain little dresser made of hard rock maple watching her in the morning light. Her long, bright hair, swept upward and held in place by tiny combs, frames her pale face reflected in the mirror. She opens her mouth, just wide enough, and careful to stay within lines I can not see, she colors her full lips with a delicious looking crayon, until they bloom, a brilliant tulip red, out of nowhere, out of a winter landscape into the vibrant spring.

Corinth, Basketball and the American Dream

If a girl who grew up on an Eagle Creek farm can have a hometown, I suppose mine would be Corinth. It was the closest place I could get to when I was a kid that had sidewalks and a movie theater. It was our postal address, too, although our mailbox on "Rural Route 2" stood in neighboring Owen County, not Grant.

As hometowns go, it fell into the tiny but ambitious category. If there had been a town square, Robert Browning's words would have been engraved on a monument: *A man's reach should exceed his grasp or what's a heaven for?* People here—and in other small towns across the country—believed in the possibilities of the American Dream. It was about trying hard enough they said. And so one day, the boys from Corinth dribbled a basketball into the headlines of America's front page, and made the town famous, if only for a moment. Because they did, those of us who came long later, grew up believing that anything was possible if we stretched our reach.

Corinth started out as a stagecoach stop on the old Covington-to-Lexington Pike, and when the railroad came calling in 1876—a magnificent line that linked Michigan to New Orleans—Corinth took off. Flushed with railroad traffic, it showed promise of becoming the region's commercial center. But bad luck plagued Corinth. Fire wiped out its downtown more than once, and it was sandwiched between two bustling county seat towns, Georgetown to the south and Williamstown to the north. By 1920, Corinth's population was only 185.

Corinth State Championship Basketball Team – 1930

Corinth High School, enrollment 74 in grades 9 – 12, won the 1930 Kentucky State Basketball Championship
and third in the 1930 National Invitational Basketball Tournament. Seated, front row, l – r: Dave Lawrence,
William Howard Jones, Ben Lawrence (brother of Dave), Roscoe Rogers, Wilber Oder. Standing, Second row,
l-r: Principal E. B. Whalen, Hugh C. McClintock, Dallas True, Eugene Ogden, John Groves, George Hayden,
and Coach Teddy Hornback.

In the late 1920s, Corinth got another chance to boom. U.S. Route 25 was built straight through the middle of the town. The fabled "Dixie Highway"—a pulsating transportation artery that linked Detroit to Augusta, Georgia—was in the vanguard of a new national highway network that would evolve into today's interstate system.

Corinth got ready for the world to come calling via its new Main Street. It had all the essentials: a handful of grocery stores and barber shops, a couple of Mom and Pop restaurants, a bootlegger and several churches, two banks, a doctor or two, a hotel, and a new two story brick high school with a gleaming gymnasium.

After U.S. 25 opened, Corinth's population jumped to 265— an increase of forty-three percent. In the fall of 1929, however, the Great Depression hit the country like an atomic bomb. Even the most optimistic Chamber of Commerce would not have dreamed the town would make headlines in the nation's newspapers six months later. As can happen in Kentucky, it was basketball that brought fame to Corinth.

Baseball may have been the national pastime, but by the 1920s, more high schools had organized basketball teams than any other sport. Perhaps that was because it could be played inside or out, in all seasons, with only five players and little equipment.

However, its popularity was due in part to Amos Alonzo Stagg, the athletic director and coach at the University of Chicago. In 1917, Stagg organized the National Interscholastic Basketball Tournament (NIBT). By 1923, Staggs' national tournament for public high school basketball teams had grown to include forty schools from all sections of the country, and had become the darling of the media.

At a time when there were no college basketball playoffs, Staggs' NIBT was the emotional equivalent of today's NCAA tournament. "Movie men" filmed portions of the games for flickering black and white newsreels. Newspapers from New York to Los Angeles shouted the names of winners and losers on their front pages in ink-bold headlines an inch high. And an exciting new phenomenon called radio broadcast all five days of the competition. On farms, in cities or small towns, Americans listened spellbound to the staccato voices of the broadcasters who brought the roundball drama into their living rooms.

By the spring of 1930, however, America was fighting for its economic life. It was expensive to send the high school teams to Chicago for such an event, and educators began to fume that the players were missing too much class time. The emerging NCAA also fretted about possible recruiting violations on the part of college coaches who were everywhere at the school boys tournament. The 1930 NIBT would turn out to be the last.

Against this backdrop, Corinth made its national debut in April 1930. By all accounts, Corinth was a team worthy of the NIBT's larger than life stage. With an enrollment of only 74 students in grades 9–12, Corinth had become the smallest school to ever win the Kentucky State High School Basketball Tournament. [*]

Corinth had entered the state tournament as what one sports writer of the era called "the darkest of dark horses." Armed only with a jump shot, it proceeded to slay one Goliath after another. First, it had to win the Class B championship for small schools where it faced Tolu in the final round. Tolu's achievements had earned it the reputation of "another Carr Creek," and it was expected to defeat Corinth easily. Corinth, however, held on for a one-point win, and emerged as the Class B Champion. Kavanaugh/Lawrenceburg had come out of a tough large school bracket, defeating an impressive Hazard team in the final game to become the Class A champion. The Kentucky state title game was then set between tiny Corinth, the Class B Champion, and Kavanaugh, the Class A winner.

The sports writers who had dismissed Corinth, and prematurely crowned Kavanaugh as Kentucky's best, were in for a surprise. The 1930 title game is described in newspaper accounts as one of the most exciting ever played in the series. With the roar of the crowd lifting the roof of the gymnasium, Corinth made three perfect shots from mid-court in thirty seconds to win by two points at the buzzer. The entire population of Corinth—watching from the bleachers or listening at home on the radio—took a breath.

As the Kentucky state champion, Corinth then qualified to compete in the NIBT, but had to pay its own way to Chicago. News articles say only that local volunteers "raised the money." I can imagine it coming in nickel and dime donations from farmers like my grandfather, Gran Hudson, who came to Corinth every Saturday afternoon to loaf. I can feel the spring rain on the

---

[*] Corinth, with an enrollment of seventy-four in grades 9–12, was the smallest school to win the Kentucky boys basketball tournament up to 1930 according to newspaper reports of the era. Eight decades later, KHSAA does not have the necessary records to determine if Corinth remains the smallest championship school. However, my informal research indicates that only the 1992 champion, University Heights, a private school that was a three-year rather than a four-year high school, was smaller.

women's faces as they carried in homemade chocolate fudge and apple pies to the bake sales before the exhibition games. The Corinth Deposit Bank surely would have donated a hundred dollars.

I can't find out if the team traveled by Greyhound bus or by train to the Windy City. I only know who went: first year Coach Teddy Hornback, team captain Frank "Bear" Lawrence and his brother Dave, and the other starting players, Roscoe Rogers, Wilbur Odor, and William Jones; alternates John Groves, Dallas True, Eugene Ogden, Hugh McClintock; and principal E. B. Whalin.

When they got to Chicago they played their hearts out. Against the odds, they defeated four teams from Wisconsin, Montana, Wheeling, WVA, and Savannah, GA. They lost the fifth game, but won the sixth to capture THIRD PLACE bragging rights in the nation. Folks listening in Corinth hugged their radios and wept with pride.

Hornback was named National High School Coach of the Year, and would go on to have a distinguished coaching career as an assistant to the fabled Ed Diddle at Western Kentucky University. Later he became WKU's long-time Athletic Director.

Dave Lawrence[**] caught the eye of the newly hired young coach at the University of Kentucky. Lawrence would play on Adolph Rupp's first teams—making Corinth folks UK fans for generations. He served as the Wildcats team captain and was All-SEC first team.

Today, Corinth's population holds steady at 181. Forty years ago, the new interstate veered to the west and now old Dixie Highway is as quiet as a country lane. The fine brick high school and its proud gymnasium have long since been torn down and the ground seeded in bluegrass. But people here remember.

[**] Dave Lawrence is listed as an All-American in several sources, but UK official records do not include him on UK's roster of All-American players.

Go Big Blue

Every year I come down with a case of March Madness. You see, I absolutely love the University of Kentucky men's basketball team. If my Wildcats get knocked out of the running early for the championship, the salt goes out of living. If they do well in tournament play, euphoria lifts my flat feet until I fancy I could dance on rooftops.

The funny thing about this obsession is that I know next to nothing about other major sports. While my peers were paying attention and learning the rules of football, baseball, tennis and golf, I had my head stuck in a novel.

I also have a low kinetic I. Q. That's educator-speak for the clumsy students who get chosen last for playground teams. I actually flunked the vocational-physical aptitude test that the state Department of Education administered to high school seniors, and The Commonwealth of Kentucky declared me too uncoordinated for unskilled factory work.

Remembering the old adage that those who can't do, teach, I set off for college. But for the mercy of C. M. Newton, I might not have graduated, at least not with my grade point average intact. C. M. went on to fame and fortune as a Division 1 basketball coach and big-time athletic director, but he got his start at tiny Transylvania where he had to cope with the likes of me in mandatory physical education classes. Despite my dismal performance in four different sports over four semesters, he gave me A minuses anyway. Extra credit, he said, for never cutting classes, showing up early and dressed to play, and for something he called my good attitude. That could be code for groveling, but I prefer to think that Coach Newton saw past my physical awkwardness into my basketball loving soul.

203

However, according to an article in *Psychology Today* by Dr. Allen R. McConnell, my klutziness could be the reason I'm a Wildcat fan-atic. He writes that fans like me are Basking in Reflected Glory or as he phrases it, BIRGing. And I admit that when one of the Cats dribbles all the way down the court in a nanosecond and slam dunks the basket, I BIRG quite a bit. For a moment, I feel kinetically gifted as if this old body had soared in the air too.

Although I don't have the degrees in psychology that Dr. McConnell has, I would suggest that BIRTHing, rather than BIRGing turned me into a Wildcat basketball fan. Daddy and his four tall, lanky brothers claimed my heart for roundball long before I was born and smudged my DNA with Kentucky Blue.

With a full family team, Daddy and the Uncles took on all comers in the barnyard league, playing pickup ball wherever someone had hung a hoop. For a decade or more, the Green Brothers were also a force on the old New Liberty High School team. The late Bud Stamper—who attended nearby Owenton High—told me about breathing a sigh of relief "the year the Green boy graduated."

"Then, lo and behold, the next season here came another Green boy. This went on for years, always another Green," he said. I had trouble convincing him there were only five brothers and not a dozen as he insisted.

Daddy and the Uncles came of age in the 1930s when a young coach named Adolph Rupp was beginning to build the University of Kentucky into a basketball powerhouse. Rupp led UK to four NCAA championships and a bushel of other titles, and holds the second highest winning percentage in the history of college basketball coaching. Following Rupp's teams on their radios, I suspect Daddy and the Uncles did do some BIRGing. Growing up poor during the Depression in one of America's most impoverished states, UK's success made Kentucky farm boys like them proud and gave them hope that they, too, could compete, not necessarily in basketball, but in life.

They became, literally, die-hard UK fans for the rest of their lives. Uncle Woodrow, in his 80s, lay in a coma for days. Told to expect his death at any hour, the family gathered at his bedside. The UK game was playing on the TV in his hospital room, and it was a close one. Finally, UK made the winning basket at the buzzer. Five seconds later Uncle Woodrow gasped his last breath—and then coded. We all believe he put off dying until he knew how the game turned out.

My own earliest memories speak to me in the voice of Cawood Ledford who broadcast the UK games on radio for decades. Cawood's rapid-fire voice, pitched high with excitement one moment, filled with scorn for bad officiating or a player's error the next, brought Wildcat basketball into every holler in the state.

At our place, no obligation interfered with game-time. In the tobacco stripping room, in the car, or around our kitchen table, Daddy, Mother and I would mark off the winter days listening to the Wildcats. I think I saw the games more clearly on Cawood's radio than I do on today's 100-inch screens.

Dr. McConnell worries about the flip side of BIRGing, the loss of self-esteem when a fan's team loses as my Cats sometimes do in important games. I would tell him about the night in 1957 when Daddy and I had standing room only tickets in old Memorial Coliseum to see UK play Temple. It turned out to be what reporters then called "the longest game in UK history." Kentucky's Hatton hit an amazing 47-foot shot at the buzzer to tie the regulation game. UK eventually defeated Temple by 2 points but in a triple overtime.

Even though my feet were hurting, I learned a lot about not giving up that night. There's always a chance to prevail, if not now then next season, and that's not a bad way to live a life.

Snow White

I spent my prime, as Miss Jean Brody said, directing amateur school plays. Perhaps that's why my heart went out to the Japanese theater arts teacher I read about in a recent news item. The principal ordered her to cast every child in the role of Snow White, the main character in the fifth grade musical. With the self-esteem of a generation hanging in the balance—not to mention his job—the principal caved in to pressure from parents. He decreed that Snow White and the Seven Dwarfs would be All Stars and Nobody Else and told the drama teacher (politely of course) to lump her own self-esteem issues. "So what?" he said, if she's a laughing stock in thespian circles.

The parents argued it was only fair that each child know the thrill of being Snow White. Imagine the stigma of being cast as one of the dwarfs, they pointed out. And for the children marginalized in the chorus as butterflies and birds—who can project what damage that might do to a child's confidence?

The article was stingy on details. I wondered how the director got thirty Snow Whites on stage at the same time? Did she cue them up in a row and have them read the lines in unison? Or maybe one Snow White flitted out to recite a line, exited stage left, as another princess whirled on stage right and said the next? But oh my—how did the director keep all those giggling princesses quiet in the wings? I wondered, too, how the fifth grade boys felt about playing Snow White, but maybe being the star of the show supersedes gender issues.

As for the rest of the characters in the play—well, I'm guessing the director cast the school faculty in those parts. The principal would bring the house down in the role of Dopey. The PE teacher could be cast against type as Sleepy. The language arts teachers, already marginalized, would fit right into the chorus as butterflies and birds. And who better to play the despised stepmother-witch than the director herself?

For all my kidding around, I confess that I, too, have known the pain of not being the star of the show. The first play I auditioned for was the seventh grade musical, Bethany Elementary's adaptation of *The Adventures of Tom Sawyer*. I desperately wanted to play the role of Becky Thatcher, the female lead who was Tom's girlfriend. It was not to be.

For starters, Becky had to sing numerous solos, and I couldn't carry a tune in a bucket. I also didn't have long blonde curls like pretty Linda Wright who won the part. But I think what really knocked me out of the running was my height. I was a good foot taller than Jimmy Gibson, the boy who was born to play Tom Sawyer.

I was assigned the non-singing role of the Old Maid neighbor. As Miss Watson, I wouldn't get to dress up pretty like Becky Thatcher. My hair would be powdered gray, and I'd have to wear a dowdy old woman's dress and ugly shoes. And even though I was a whiz at memorizing, I only had one short line to learn—"That's what I say."

Miss Watson wasn't even close to being a plum part, but I didn't want to be left out, so I swallowed my pride and showed up at rehearsals for two months. The only upside, in my opinion, was that Miss Watson was onstage in quite a few scenes, and got to repeat "that's what I say" as a refrain throughout the script.

At last, opening night arrived, and our production lumbered onstage. Imagine my surprise when Miss Watson made the audience laugh out loud each time I piped in with "That's what I say." I hadn't known that she—or I—could be funny, or that her character was important in moving the plot along. My Miss Watson was a hit—if not a star—and I was glad I'd ended up in that part. I even felt relief that I didn't have to squeak through Becky Thatcher's solos.

That night, in my childish way, I began to understand that being the star may not be any more important than being a hit in a supporting role. I saw that it takes the entire cast to make a good show. Each person, onstage and backstage, is essential. Without everyone doing their part, the play would be one-dimensional and dull as dirt. So it is in life. If everyone's a star then nothing gets done. It's all noise and chaos. It's a boring fashion show of egos posturing in beautiful costumes.

And so I would hope all children get a chance to play Miss Watson—that they have the chance to become someone they didn't know they wanted to be, to discover abilities they didn't know they had. I would hope all children could be a hit in life—if not the star of the show.

Touch the Stars

Annelise wants to be a spaceman, she told me, so that she and I can fly to the moon.

"What will we do when we get there?" I asked, not telling her that the astronauts had found the moon to be a cold, dark place. I sank deeper into my easy chair, though, in case she had any ill-timed illusions of leaving the earth's atmosphere that afternoon. My bones have been achy lately, and I wasn't sure I was up to spur of the moment space travel.

She answered matter-of-factly as though the answer would be obvious if I weren't so old between the ears.

"When we get to the moon, we can touch the stars," she said.

A few weeks later, our family took off to Disney World, in part to celebrate Annelise's fourth birthday. It wasn't exactly a trip to the moon, but it was a journey to a different sphere. And when Mickey Mouse and Donald Duck dropped by her party, I knew from the reflection in her eyes that we were touching the stars.

Despite a week sprinkled with stardust, I confess I was looking forward to our first day back home as we drove north to Kentucky. It may be that only a mother of a certain age can appreciate how joyful it is to have all her adult children, in-laws, and grandchildren together, much less together at Disney World. But it may be that only a mother of a certain age can appreciate how exhausting such joy can be. Our clan numbers thirteen now, with one more on the way, and our ages range from decrepit— that would be me—to our youngest grandchild who is 18 months old. Our personalities and temperaments are as diverse as that age span would suggest, and a week of 24/7 togetherness is about as much as our love for each other can embrace.

Thoughts of a good night's sleep on our king-sized Tempur-Pedic mattress helped me ignore swollen feet and the chronic pain in my left buttock as the car chugged its way up I-75. By the time we crossed the Tennessee border, I was mentally drawing a hot bath in my big tub. I could almost feel Calgon's blue bubbles resting under my chin.

When we finally pulled into our Lexington driveway, I was out of the car the instant my husband turned off the motor. I dashed into the house, pausing only long enough to release my poor feet from those hateful athletic shoes, and headed towards our first floor bedroom and its adjacent bath to get the water running in the tub.

When my bare feet hit the back hall, however, they sank into cold, wet carpet. Could I be hallucinating? Was I already in the bath? Why wasn't it hot?

Then reason took over. I sucked in my breath and made myself walk on. Sure enough, water was spewing from our commode's cut-off valve like a tiny geyser as though it thought it might turn into Old Faithful if it tried hard enough.

I yelled for Ernie to come and look. I think I was hoping he would tell me it was an illusion, like one of the 3-D movies we'd seen at Disney World. Instead, he stood there in the sort of silence that screams of having lived enough years to know what this meant.

"Let's go take a look at the basement," he finally said.

We were greeted at the top of the stairs by an unfamiliar musty odor. My stomach did one of those somersault things it used to do when I was a kid afraid in the dark.

By the time we reached the bottom of the stairs, I could hear water dripping onto stone, a sound I associated with a visit I once made to Mammoth Cave. Ernie flipped on the lights, and for a moment I thought I might be in a cave. Water was dripping from the ceiling in random abandon, puddling in pools on the furniture like a rude guest who's never heard of using coasters.

On the over-sized—okay, in my opinion gorgeous and unique—coffee table we'd discovered at a sale some years ago and carefully transported home in the back of our SUV.

On the mahogany inlaid console table—the one our daughter has asked us to leave her in the will—that stands behind the leather sofa holding a lamp.

And of course on the ceramic tile floor. Water stretched thirty feet or more from one side of the open basement area to the other. All the chair legs, upholstered and otherwise, were wading in it.

I studied the two matching area rugs that I'd spent weeks of my life selecting and ordering to specific sizes to fit the odd dimensions of our space. When I bent to feel them they gave way to my touch like giant saturated sponges.

A familiar ache moved from my lower back to my knee to my ankle, and I longed to sit down. And so I did. I waded across the clear lake that my basement family room had become, found a mostly dry chair, and plopped down.

That's when Ernie said, "It could have been worse."

"Yes, it could have been a hurricane," I replied. I confess that a reasonable person would have heard sarcasm in my voice.

But Ernie was on a roll. "We could be homeless tonight, but we still have the upstairs guest room to sleep in."

He went on. "And there's no water in the main floor family room or kitchen or dining room."

And that's when I noticed the quilts, the ancient ones hand pieced by Ernie's mother and grandmother, so exquisite and fragile that we've hung them on the two opposing walls of the basement family room like the works of art they surely are. The water dripping through the ceiling had not reached to the edges of the large room. The quilts had been spared.

I remembered then that even on the moon—actually a cold, dark place the astronauts reported—you have to look if you want to see the stars, reach if you expect to touch them.

"Okay," I finally said. "Who should we call to help us fix this?"

Baby Hudson

Hudson Alexander Brown, two days old, came home on the first day of spring. He has the look of a reasonable boy about the eyes. Leastwise, we were able to talk some sense into him when he took a notion to get born in mid-January.

"Look," we said. "If you have a choice, you shouldn't pick a birthday two weeks after Christmas. People are tired and broke then, and in Kentucky old man winter can dump a blizzard on your party without so much as a warning on the 11 o'clock news."

Right on cue, an ice storm shut down the state and over a million people lost electric power. He took our point.

Nevertheless, he tried an end run again in February.

"Have you considered that this is the height of the flu season," we reminded him as the doctors gave him steroid shots to strengthen his lungs. "If this were the Olympics," we went on (as we are wont to do) "you'd already be disqualified for using performance enhancing drugs."

But he was only teasing us, he claims now, and in the end he had the last laugh. He was born only a few days before his due date and weighed a whopping nine pounds six ounces.

He is our fifth grandchild and our third grandson. He is his parents' second child.

Being a latecomer in the family lineup can be an advantage, we tell him, can take the pressure off, and give him space to develop his game at his own pace without all of us second-guessing his every move. The coaching staff he's inherited has improved over time, too.

True, his grandfather and I are not as peppy as we were ten years ago when our first grandson was born, but we have the

212

benefit of experience now (and we also have a better camera.) Even his parents are more relaxed and confident than they were two and a half years ago when they brought his sister, Annelise, home.

"Remember who you are," I wrote when she was born, reminding her that she was born into a family that recycles love and enduring values from generation to generation. Lest her brother ever be tempted to forget who he is, his parents have given him a name that will remind him. The Hudson is for my mother and her people, the Alexander after his father. It's a big name with a lot of history for both sides of his family, and I think it fit for a governor—or at least a rock star.

Or a butcher, a baker, a candlestick maker—I don't really care, Hudson, as long as you become as good a man as you can be. I'm hoping you'll be the sort who doesn't laugh when others fall down; who doesn't get mad and quit trying when you lose at something; who doesn't pitch a fit to get your own way regardless of the cost to others.

On this spring morning, I'd give you world peace if I could, prosperity and the moon thrown into the bargain, and a world free from cancer. I'd give you happiness every moment of your life.

But I know I can't promise to deliver on any of those gifts. I can only try to teach you to live in personal peace, to prepare yourself to earn a living, to reach as high as the moon though it may exceed your grasp, to lead a healthy lifestyle. I can't make you happy, but I can encourage you to learn how to make yourself happy.

I can promise though—as I did to your sister and your cousins—to remember who I am as I commence my peripheral role in your journey to adulthood. It is I who must not forget the wisdom, the strength, and the love passed hand over hand from one generation to the next.

So happy birthday, Baby Hudson. The gift I bring to your party may be recycled, but it's the best I have to give. I give you what was given to me.

Leon Harris

His name popped up in my email with uncanny timing. I was deep into planning the eightieth reunion of The Rev. Silas A. Hudson's descendants, and a few days earlier, I'd been to see *The Help*, a movie about racial prejudice encountered by black domestic workers circa 1963 Mississippi. You see, Leon R. Harris (1886-1960) was a black writer who spent most of his childhood living in my white g-g-grandfather's Kentucky home. Leon's words reach across the decades to tell me how it felt to be Silas Hudson's "help."

A mulatto, Harris says he was treated "like a white boy" by Silas Hudson. Most in the farm community, however, even some of Hudson's family, kept him (in his words) in "the nigger boy's world." He was happiest alone, in the woodshed, where he could hide and read, he says. Hearing his words echo across a century, I blush. With pride for the Hudsons' small contribution to this man's success? With shame for the pain he endured despite my family's fumbling efforts to do-good? I'm not sure.

Dr. John Garst, professor emeritus at the University of Georgia, contacted me by email. "I am doing research and writing a book on John Henry, the steel-driving man, a legendary figure in American folklore. In 1927, Leon Harris provided an important text of the song, 'John Henry.' In looking into Leon Harris' background, I find that he went from an orphanage in Cambridge, Ohio ... to live with the Silas Hudson family, where he is found in the census of 1900.... Do you know anything about all of this?"

"Well, yes," I replied. "Harris was mythic in our family stories."

G-Aunt Lilly Hudson, Silas Hudson's strong-willed unmarried daughter, "got it in her head," they said, to take in an eight-year-old black orphan to "help" with work in the house. An extra pair of hands in a rural 19th century household that included her elderly parents and her bachelor brother would have been appealing. Most local people, however, seeking "help" in exchange for room and board took in poor white children from nearby.

Aunt Lilly, though, was a devout and intelligent woman, influenced by the philanthropic movements of the late 1800s. Approaching thirty and childless, I suspect she emphasized her need for "help" to deflect criticism for taking in a black child to raise. In the 1890s, after all, the Civil War was still being fought in whispers in southern-leaning Owen County.

Lilly's orphan turned out to be bright and personable, and an eager student who delighted her father, Silas Hudson, a country lawyer and an ordained minister. The way my grandfather, George Hudson, told the story to me more than a half century later, Leon "was treated like a member of the family" in Silas' home. Defying local attitudes, Silas insisted that the child eat all his meals at the table with them, and on Sunday mornings, Aunt Lilly ruffled feathers by seating the little boy beside her on the piano bench at the front of the Methodist church as she played for the congregation. "I need Leon to turn the pages of the hymnal," she said.

Eighty-something Silas Hudson was so highly regarded in the community that no one dared challenge him directly for bringing a black child into his family circle. But people criticized him behind his back, and a lifetime later, my grandfather was still defensive on his grandfather's behalf. Gran Hudson would boast with an in-their-face attitude about Leon's education, of his work as a well-paid railroader during the depression, even of his writing poetry though I suspect my grandfather never read a poem in his life.

Yet, when Harris came to visit our home in the summer of 1952, my grandfather did not invite him inside. He greeted him with warmth and courtesy at the door and then, after standing for a few minutes talking, asked him to sit with him on our wide front porch. In an era before air conditioning we often sat with warm weather guests outside, and so this did not seem unusual to me. The two old men sat together for an hour or two, talking and laughing, enjoying each other.

Leon Harris at the Hudson Family Reunion, 1952

Later that day, though, I overheard my mother criticize Gran Hudson, out of his hearing. She knew that he had been reluctant to invite a black man into his home as a guest, and had not uttered the automatic "Come in!" that was ingrained in our family's good manners. It's a glimpse of my kind grandfather at variance with all other images. I remind myself that he was born only a dozen years after the Civil War ended, that there were still segregated fountains and restrooms at the Owen County Court-house in 1952. Yet "come in" lingers unspoken, an unwelcome ghost haunting my memories.

I am indebted to John Garst for the rest of Harris' story. I have learned that his accomplishments were even greater than my grandfather realized. I understand, too, that Gran didn't have a clue how young Leon felt clinging to the outside of the only family he had.

According to Harris, he "ran away from the white folks" when he was rising fourteen. His autobiographical novel suggests that he left soon after a bad fight with one of Hudson's grandsons who taunted him. The fight didn't sit well with some of Silas' sons. Walking and hitchhiking seventy-five miles, he arrived at Berea College where he presented himself with a letter of recommendation from Aunt Lilly, his "private teacher." He enrolled as a work-study student in the fall of 1900, but the infamous Day Law that would eventually prevail in closing integrated classrooms at Berea, nudged him on to Booker T. Washington's Tuskegee Institute in Alabama by the fall of 1901. He studied there for three years and made influential friends. By 1915 he was listed in *Who's Who of the Colored Race.*

He worked at teaching, lecturing, farming, in steel mills and for the railroad—"because he had to eat," he said—but writing was his passion, and he used this to help his people. He published numerous magazine articles and was editor and publisher of several black newspapers. He was co-founder and president of the National Federation of Colored Farmers, active in the NAACP at the state and national level, served on President Hoover's Committee On Negro Housing, and corresponded with the likes of W. E. B. Du Bois, Martin Luther King, Jr., and Thurgood Marshall. He published three volumes of poetry, and of course collected and published an important version of the ballad, "John Henry."

He also wrote an autobiographical novel, *Run Zebra Run*. A contemporary account of race relations at the turn of the last century, it has been discovered by academics and included in black studies curriculum. The cheapest copy I could locate on the internet sold for $300, with some copies going for $600. So I rely on John Garst who has read it, and on Internet commentaries. It seems that Silas comes off well, but my g-g-grandmother did not. She's described as coming "from a ... backward family ... [who] aims to keep the 'little nigger' in his place." Harris is graphic in his description of the verbal abuse and prejudices his young orphaned protagonist, "Leonard Hall" encounters in the household of "Silas Harker."

The day after Leon Harris visited our home in 1952, he attended the Hudson Reunion. My father, Dexter Green, was presiding president that year, and he asked Leon to give the invocation. Harris responded with a prayer he had learned from old Silas. They were the same words I'd heard my grandfather, Gran Hudson, repeat at our table nearly every meal of my life.

> Our Father, accept our thanks
> For these and our many blessings,
> Pardon and forgive our sins,
> And save us—

Householders

My husband says he'd rather watch paint dry. The pace is faster. And even I admit the cheerful narrator of "Househunters" looks and sounds like a Stepford Wife. "Will they choose house number one with the crummy kitchen, house number two with the awful yard, or house number three that mortgages their soul?" she asks, showing all her teeth without a crease in her smile. And yet, I can't turn the TV off when "Househunters" comes on.

I'm mesmerized week after week as eager buyers set out to find a home that matches their budget and their dreams. For one thing, I feel smug because I live in beautiful Kentucky where an ugly one-bedroom bungalow doesn't cost a million dollars. But mostly I watch because I've learned so much about buying houses over a lifetime. I could tell the householders on TV a thing or two if they'd only listen.

Ten years ago this week, we moved to our current place, the one I'll call the October House. It wasn't love at first sight, but we were exhausted with the search, and we needed a good shower. More precisely, we needed enough showers to accommodate our three twenty-something daughters when they all came home and wanted to wash their hair at the same time.

The price and the location were right, and its good bones trumped its shortcomings. We could make it work. We'd owned four houses prior to the October House, and we'd learned that there's more to a good real estate match than passion.

We'd been wildly infatuated with our first house, a trendy A-frame. We bought it the early spring, not long before our first wedding anniversary when we were still green behind the ears. It had been abused by a leaky roof and the previous owners' bad taste, but we were captivated by the deep, wooded lot where deer sometimes came to nibble. I had visions of building a tree house for our unborn children, a tree house so magnificent that even our grandchildren would cherish it in time. And we'd become famous thereabouts, too, for the live white pine, twelve feet tall, we'd mount each Christmas in the tall living room. But despite the charm of our soaring ceiling—not to mention Bambi scampering on the lawn—in a few years, we fell out of love with our two-bedroom, one bath cottage.

Our heads were turned by a pretty ranch with more bedrooms and a huge playroom in the basement. We signed the contract on a hot summer day, and I figured we'd live there forever. I even saw myself writing a Pulitzer Prize winning novel at the kitchen table looking out over the child-friendly back yard.

We did stay for a good long stretch though I never got around to much writing. Our three girls pretty much grew up in that house, and we worked it near to death. Then in its dowdy middle age, we ran off and left it for an affair with a dream house.

A three story brick Georgian with a park-like lawn, the dream house was all we'd ever wanted. I envisioned forever again—the weddings we'd have there and the crannies where the grandchildren would play. And yet, we learned that it can be difficult living up to a dream. For example, can you eat pizza straight out of the box in a dream family room? Should you dress up a little for morning coffee in the dream breakfast room?

When job changes took us to another city five years later and with our last child off to college, we decided to be practical—for the sake of pizza I think. Anyway, I remember we ate pizza hot from the box on our January moving-in day. The cute sort-of-Victorian we had bought was perfect for empty nesters. Forever had started seeming shorter to me by then, and I stopped thinking about it as much.

But the Empty-Nester was shy on showers, and to our surprise, our nest didn't feel as empty as we'd expected. First one son-in-law and then another showed up and then, of course, a grandchild. That's when we went hunting for the October House.

Its two walls of bookcases in the front room charmed me despite the ugly paint on the walls. I thought I might be able to write in such a house, and I have (though no Pulitzers loom on the horizon.) Deer don't graze in the citified backyard, but we do see plenty of squirrels and rabbits. The sub-division lawn isn't zoned for a grand tree house, either. But the high back deck— built by some sensitive soul around ancient locust trees, saving them—sort of feels like one, and our grandchildren love to play out there. The great room's tall ceiling even accommodates a 10-foot Christmas tree. It's artificial, but we can put it up the week after Thanksgiving, and it's famous within our family if not the city.

And we've had a wedding or two while living here. We've grieved, too, for friends and loved ones lost, but we have good memories of Mother and the others sitting around our holiday table in the October House.

After a decade, I realize with surprise that we might live here forever. Then again, we may not. And so if I could make the anxious househunters inside my TV hear me, I'd tell them what Mother once said to me.

Except for a handful of years at the end of her life, Mother lived all her days on the farm where she was born, land her ancestors settled on in the 1830s. She valued place and permanence. When I once complained to her, however, that my family and I wouldn't have the same sense of home she had known, her reprimand came quick.

"Home is not a house, but the people in the house," she said.

Remember that forever, I would add.

Ernie

Bird Watching

In the fifth grade, I often stayed up long after my parents had gone to bed, making sure the margins in my geography notebook were straight as an arrow for Miz Eva Lois Wright. This genetic disposition to please people now obliges me to respond quickly to the plethora of "Getting To Know You" quizzes my friends have taken to sending me on the Internet.

The questionnaires are similar to the icebreaker games of my Methodist Youth Fellowship days, silly and sort of fun. Most of us, though, have known each other so long we can recite each other's grade school crushes in chronological order. Still, it can be surprising to learn what a lifelong friend actually eats for breakfast.

And I admit that some of the questions make me stop and think. For example, a recent quiz wanted to know if I were a bird watcher? An image of Dick Davenport in a pith helmet leaped to mind. He was the obsessive ornithologist married to Congressman Lacey Davenport in the Doonesbury comic strip. You may not remember him because Trudeau killed him off with a massive heart attack in 1986—at the very moment Davenport finally snapped a photo of the rare and elusive Bachman's Warbler.

So no, I'm not a bird watcher, not with binoculars, not with a camera, not in a safari outfit purchased at Banana Republic. But living as I do in the middle of a bunch of trees, I do see a lot of birds.

For example, our four-year-old grandson Owen spotted a hummingbird on our deck this weekend, and talked incessantly about it for the rest of the day. I share Owen's enthusiasm. A

223

hummingbird—the bird that isn't engineered to fly at all—is one of God's most inspiring creations.

I'm fond, too, of the cheerful red cardinals that bathe in our fountain. They remind me of my mother-in-law who lived on a street called Cardinal Court for the last fifteen years of her life. She loved the color red, too, and so began collecting red cardinal figurines. When I see the red birds out our window, I fancy she's sent them to say hello from heaven.

The greedy blue jays fight with the chipmunks for whatever bounty falls in our yard. They make me think of Mark Twain's funny old story, the one about the blue jay who hoarded nuts, dropping them one by one down a knothole in the roof of an empty cabin. He drove himself crazy trying to fill the hole up to the top.

And nobody could ignore the gossipy pigeons who come waddling across the deck like Russian babushkas in headscarves and short fur coats. They're always prepared for winter and for the worst. The mourning doves stop by occasionally too. They remind me of puffed up, stuffy old men, maybe undertakers. They make me sad wailing as they do.

But I'm infatuated with a graceful yellow finch that favors a branch growing near our front bow window. I stare at this exquisite black and yellow creature, and I remember the feeling of being young, of feeling pretty and flitting, however briefly, like a bird.

Robins aren't beautiful in the way of the yellow finch, but they're cute, the way cheerleaders used to be before they got mixed up with the Dallas Cowboys. The robins remind me of the old song that went bob, bob, bobbing along waking up sleepyheads when I was a little girl. Why don't people sing that fine song anymore?

Occasionally a giant blue heron perches on my neighbors' roof stalking the fish in their koi pond. I stop and admire the heron's magnificence and its power even as I pity its prey.

And every day, I watch the birds foul the lime-green umbrellas that shade the tables on my deck. They do this with abandon, and I suspect, with a giggle. Even as I go through my daily cleaning of the umbrellas, though, I admire the birds' ability to adapt to changing circumstances, to persist and survive. Less than twenty years ago, my city sub-division was somebody's tobacco farm. Interstate 75, a couple of miles from my back yard, now carries a ga-zillion cars from north to south across America. Man O War Boulevard, one of the major routes through Lexington, is even closer, and houses stretch away in all directions. Yet the birds have adapted to this shifting landscape.

His eye is on the sparrow, I remember hearing. Would that His eye be on me as I learn from the birds.

Pat and Me

There are two kinds of people in the world. Well, there are a lot more than that, but for the purposes of telling this story, there are only two, Pat and me.

Like Mutt and Jeff, we were physical opposites. Pat was a short, tan brunette and spoke in a full, loud, voice. I was a tall, pale blonde and people were always asking me to "speak up" because I talked so softly.

Pat was impulsive and gregarious. Give her five minutes' notice and a pound of baloney, and she'd whip up a party. I was deliberate, more at ease with a good book in those days than in a room full of people. And when I hosted a gathering it took days of preparation to meet my self-imposed standards of perfection.

I was shocked when Pat told me she never folded her underwear, just stuffed it into a drawer. I didn't know you could do that. I thought there was a law. I kept a surplus in my bank account and Pat—well, you get the idea. What is important is that Pat chose me to be her friend when I was a twenty-two year old homesick bride transplanted to an unfamiliar town hours away from my home.

I'm unsure what attracted Pat to me. She confided that she'd been an insecure student in college so maybe my bookishness impressed her. I could make her laugh with my young teacher tales of woe in the classroom, and I was a good listener, too, who enjoyed her stories about family and childrearing and neighborhood gossip. Maybe, though, it was only my availability in a small place new to both of us that brought us together.

Whatever, I'm sure I took more from Pat than she did from me. A few years older, she filled in for the big sister I didn't have, and helped me navigate in the new grown-up world of work and marriage I'd stumbled into. She taught me practical things like how to pinch geranium blossoms when they wither to get them to bloom again and how to make beef stroganoff with hamburger instead of sirloin.

One October morning several years into our friendship, Pat called as she often did, with a spur of the moment invitation. Her car was scheduled for repairs at the Chevrolet Garage in Huntington, West Virginia, twenty miles away. Come with her, she said. The dealership's van would take us downtown to shop while the car was being serviced. I was pregnant with our first child and feeling rocky, and Pat had a three year old son named Jimmy and no babysitter, so on the face of it, this was a silly idea. But this was way before there was a shopping mall on every corner, and the prospect of shopping in the middle of the week in downtown Huntington sounded like an excursion to us.

The dealership's blue van dropped us in front of Stone & Thomas Department Store, and we made arrangements with the driver to meet at the same place at four o'clock. We had a wonderful day. We had lunch in the tearoom on the third floor. I shopped for maternity clothes. Pat found an outfit, too, and bunch of things for Jimmy.

At four o'clock, we stationed ourselves on the street, our arms full of packages, and waited for our ride. Minutes passed. Jimmy began to cry and insisted on being held. We took turns holding either him or the stash of packages, passing off to each other in an awkward relay.

Thirty minutes had passed when it began to rain. We scurried for shelter under the roof's overhang.

An hour passed. Hunkered against the building out of the rain, I allowed as how I might need to throw up at any moment and for Pat to be prepared. Then Jimmy did throw up.

Fearing we'd been forgotten, Pat went seeking a pay phone to call the Chevrolet Garage. She returned and reported, "The van is on its way. Traffic must have delayed it, they said."

At that very moment, the blue van pulled up to the curb. "Hooray," we shouted, splashing through puddles of standing rainwater, as we dashed towards the vehicle. I flung open the back door with my free hand, and Pat climbed in and settled our packages in the seat behind her. I handed Jimmy (who by now refused to walk at all) up to her, and then climbed in myself and slammed the heavy door.

"Are we ever glad to see you," Pat said. "We'd just about given up on you."

I chimed in with something inane about how long we'd been standing there in the rain, but still we'd had a good time, and this sure was a nice service the dealership offered.

The van driver didn't start the motor. He didn't say anything either. He only stared at us.

After a long minute of strange silence, I asked, "You are from the Chevrolet Garage, right?"

"No mam. I'm here to pick up my wife when she gets off her shift at Stone & Thomas."

Pat and I went into reverse, climbing out of the van into the pouring rain, with our arms full of packages, with Jimmy, with embarrassment—and finally with explosions of laughter that erupted again and again against all efforts to pull ourselves together. When the garage's blue van pulled up five minutes later, we were still laughing so hard we couldn't explain our-selves to the puzzled young driver.

Eight years later, on a hot, cloudless April afternoon, Pat accepted a spur of the moment invitation to go for a joy ride in a private airplane. It crashed in a wooded area of southeastern Ohio, and she and her husband and their youngest child were killed—instantly, I hope. The wreckage, however, was not found for a week.

When word went out that Pat's plane was missing, I arrived at the house before most others did. No one would peep in her underwear drawers, I knew, but they would be bringing food in for her children and the arriving out-of-town relatives.

And so I cleaned out Pat's refrigerator from top to bottom with baking soda water. I sponged up an odd brown liquid in the vegetable drawer and tossed a casserole on the brink. I scrubbed and wiped that fridge until it sparkled, cleaning as though Pat's survival hinged on my effort to sort and organize and clean.

My obsessiveness wouldn't, couldn't, save Pat. She was al-ready gone. Now I'm old enough to draw Social Security and Pat has been dead for over thirty years. To this day, I'm not sure whether Pat would have turned down a chance to take a ride in an airplane on a beautiful April day even if she'd known she wouldn't come back.

And sometimes, I think cleaning that refrigerator was the silliest thing I've ever done. Sometimes, I think maybe it's the nicest thing I've ever done. Depends on which kind of person you are, I guess.

A Tale of Two Autumns

The first autumn I was there, it was 1976. Jimmy Carter and Gerald Ford both wanted to be elected President of the United States. I only wanted a little break from 24/7 motherhood. I wanted to walk through the soft leaves in the gorgeous fall light.

I was pregnant with our third daughter—my third pregnancy in less than five years—and my husband had urged me to come with him on a business trip to Washington. This was not routine for us. He usually traveled quick and light and with other businessmen. But this time he would be going alone, he said, and there would be time enough to drive. We would chart a scenic fall route from our home in eastern Kentucky through the mountains of West Virginia. Come along, he'd said—the leaves will be at the peak of their color.

Perhaps he sensed that the months ahead would be among the most challenging of my life. Certainly, he knew that caring for three pre-school children would be harder for me than for two. But surely, he could not have foreseen that the winter of '77 would be one of the worst in Kentucky's history. The winter of '77 is another story though. For whatever reasons, he encouraged me to come with him in October to Washington. We will remember this trip, he seemed to say without saying so.

He was right, of course. I've visited Washington in all seasons of the year. I know that. I try to count the times I've been there. I try to recall what time of the year those trips were made. But in the end, it's no use. In my memory, Washington is always bathed in fall light, always painted in autumn colors.

The company had arranged for us to stay at a quiet, refined hotel in Georgetown. Outside, a black, monogrammed canopy and wide, brick steps invited us into the polished interior. I stepped out of my world of diapers and McDonalds' cheeseburgers into those elegant surroundings without missing a beat. I was a natural sophisticate, my husband said, smiling at me with his brown eyes.

After our arrival, we were entertained for dinner at an expensive restaurant nearby. I spotted a TV celebrity across the dining room, but pretended I didn't see him as though I bumped into famous people every day. The next morning, with my husband off to important meetings, I was on my own. I decided to take a walk.

It was such a warm fall day when I stepped out of the hotel lobby that I impulsively ran back to the room, and left my sweater. Setting off finally for my walk, I ambled around the first corner and spotted a storefront filled with Carter-for-President paraphernalia. It could have been a Norman Rockwell painting. Thousands of yellow leaves, some on the street tree branches, some wafting downward in the air, framed the hand-lettered CARTER on the window. The morning sunlight pierced the leaves and bounced off the glass in prisms.

It was an omen, I decided, and so I went in and bought a Carter button. My husband is a Republican, and I knew he would wrinkle his nose at my purchase, but I decided to push the envelope in our lifelong political argument. I think I still have that button somewhere.

I felt cosmopolitan walking around alone in Georgetown. I poked my head into one pricey shop and then another as casually as I moved from produce to frozen foods in the Kroger store back home in Ashland, Kentucky. As if I did this everyday, I glided from window to window assessing tie-dyed scarves, hand thrown pottery, the patina on dark antiques, designer clothing, books, gourmet coffee.

I was intoxicated with Georgetown's tree-lined streets swaddled in jewel colored velvet leaves. I fell in love with the classic lines of its Georgian buildings, simple and elegant, and decided this was the only proper way for houses and shops to look. Ashland, Kentucky, was a raw, industrial town hunched in the mountains, and to me, on that day, it could have existed on another planet from this enchanted place. I felt young and empowered in Washington. Life lay ahead of me.

Twenty-five years later, in 2001, I returned to Washington in the fall. We'd come to move our daughter from the house she shared with her husband to an apartment she would live in alone.

We tried to be calm and nonchalant, but she'd narrowly escaped the terrorists' planes of death, and we were changed. We were afraid. Our new fear hung awkwardly on us like clothes that were too large. We looked at everyone with suspicion, in restaurants, on the sidewalks, but averted our eyes before we made eye contact. We pulled our sweaters close around us like body armor, and walked quickly, but the dry, fallen leaves snapped beneath our feet, and we started at the sound. It would have been so easy to kill us. Any fool could see that. But we came and went faking bravado. I thought of Londoners in the Blitz.

And our daughter was so fragile. We understood when we touched her that there was no room for even one small misstep on our part. She looked wild-eyed and disorganized despite earnest attempts to pull herself together. I prayed for parental wisdom I knew I did not have. If I heard an answer to my prayers, it was muffled and hard for me to understand.

And so I cleaned. I began with the refrigerator and worked my way quarter inch by quarter inch from the vegetable crisper to the icemaker. I cleaned the seldom-used oven, and vacuumed out the far corners in the gleaming cabinets. I whitened the grout in the bathroom floors, and wiped the wooden window blinds one slat at a time from first floor to the third. I dusted the painted woodwork with a white glove, and polished the hardwood floors until they mirrored my face. I cleaned the house, and cleaned the house, as if in cleaning I could—do what? Restore order to the post 9/11 world? To her world?

We set up her new apartment and again, I cleaned. I cleaned the already sterile rooms until I ran smack dab out of cleaning supplies. It was an empty place despite the unpacked boxes piled to the ceiling. It was a place with no memory despite the ghosts that followed us. Still—we hung pictures and arranged the furniture in this strange new place.

And then, with darkness falling, I walked through the piles of curling, brown leaves on the street until we reached our car. My husband turned the key in the ignition, and without stopping, we tunneled straight home to Kentucky through a cold October night.

Katherine

His call came at dawn on a Monday morning in January. It caught Katherine by surprise though it was not unexpected. She was, after all, ninety-one and a half, she reminded herself, and she'd told God some time ago that she could be ready to go on a moment's notice. She did politely ask for enough time to phone her oldest daughter, Betty, who would in turn call the others, and time enough, too, to comb her hair and change into a clean gown. Then, with the dignity that marked her life, she quietly left.

Up until that morning, however, she was engaged with living because that's what you're supposed to do if you can. She kept track of her large family, encouraged them, fretted over them. Independent to the core, she lived alone, in the tidy house her late husband built for her in the 1930s, on land that had belonged to her people long before that. There, the afternoon before her death, she entertained her clan for their regular Sunday get-together. She laughed and talked and won the last game of cards she played.

Her younger daughter Sherry has been my close friend since we were schoolgirls. Perhaps that's the reason my first column for *The News-Herald* back in 2004 caught Katherine's attention. Katherine thought it was funny, and she asked Sherry to tell me that. Thus began a once removed conversation about my stories. If Katherine liked one—if it made her laugh or cry or reminded her of a similar experience she'd had—she'd tell Sherry to let me know. If she didn't comment, I knew I hadn't quite hit the mark. Over time, her responses taught me that I had to pay attention to the details of a story to get it right for Katherine.

234

Now, Sherry has given me permission to tell this story about her mother. I hope, gentle readers, that I can get it right—for Katherine.

Practical and efficient, Katherine decided as her ninetieth birthday approached that it was time to make her funeral arrangements. This needed to be seen to, as she phrased it, while she was still on her feet. If she left it up to the kids to see to after she died, they'd overspend out of grief, and there was no point in being extravagant just because you were dead.

The family was in a big way planning a ninetieth birthday party for Katherine, and preferred to focus on living, not dying. But Katherine would not be dissuaded. So one sweltering August day, the two sisters took off work and drove their mother to McDonald's Funeral Home in Owenton.

On the surface, this didn't seem too different from other shopping excursions mothers and daughters share over a lifetime. In fact, the funeral home—a 19th century white clapboard with curlicues and a wrought iron fence around the lawn—could be mistaken for an upscale boutique in a tourist town. But the women weren't there to select a prom or wedding dress or baby clothes for grandchildren. Their frozen smiles spoke the difference as they stepped across the threshold.

After other matters were taken care of, they got down to picking out the casket, and were led into a spacious showroom filled with sample models. As if they were discussing the purchase of a new car—but with less criteria to go on—Katherine and her daughters analyzed the merits and shortcomings of each one. Some were ruled out because Katherine didn't want designs on the interior or a lot of tufts. Some, however, were too plain.

The August heat and the surreal nature of their task would suffocate them from time to time, and then they'd excuse themselves, first one, and then another, to get a drink of cold water from the cooler. But finally, Katherine narrowed the selection down to two. There wasn't much difference between her choices except the one with a pinkish cast to the metal was more expensive.

"Just pick the one you like best, Mom," Betty pressed.

"It's your funeral," Sherry noted with black humor, and the three of them laughed at the old joke.

But Katherine wouldn't choose. The less expensive one would do fine, she kept saying. She liked it. No need in being extravagant, she reminded them, just because you're dead. But her eyes were fixed on the pinkish casket, and her hand kept touching it, as if encouraging her daughters to speak up for "the pink one" (as they now were calling it.)

This stalemate lasted for a good little while. Finally, Katherine threw up her hands, and said, "Oh, I can't decide. You girls will have to do it!" With that pronouncement, she hurried into the other room, dropped her slight frame onto a camelback sofa, and began fanning herself with a McDonald's Funeral Home paper fan.

Betty and Sherry looked at each other. Then they did what their mother—they thought—had asked them to do.

Sitting at her memorial service at McDonald's Funeral Home, I suddenly understood why Katherine wanted the pink one. The wallpaper wrapped the space around us in a faint, delicate pattern of pink and green stripes, and the pinkish hue of her metal casket set against those walls was beautiful. You do have to pay attention to details to get it right, I thought. It's funny, though, how you can laugh and cry at the same time staring at a casket.

Mattie

I haven't seen her in thirty years. I doubt she's still alive. Yet a month never passes that I don't think about Mattie.

We met at a Weight Watchers class in Ashland, Kentucky. I'd lost 40 post-pregnancy pounds, and fearing I would backslide, I stepped forward to become a Weight Watchers lecturer. With the fervor of the newly converted, I set out on an evangelical mission to save our chunk of Eastern Kentucky from the demons of obesity.

In fairness, I should note that our part of the state had its share of women who could walk the plank in a bikini with the best of them. Like the Duchess of Windsor they believed a woman can never be too thin or too rich. But they weren't among the potluck-loving majority. They weren't the people who'd put us on the map, dead center in what the AMA dubbed "Coronary and Gallstone Valley." At its roots, Ashland was a home-fried sort of place.

I'd been proselytizing for about six months when Mattie joined one of my classes. As I watched her sitting at the registration table filling out our ubiquitous forms, I realized that her weight would exceed the normal range of our scales. I remembered, though, that we could accommodate individuals up to 600 pounds by adapting the balance beam apparatus with additional weights. I'd never had to use them before.

Trying to be discrete, I fumbled for the seldom-used chunks of metal in the clutter of our supply boxes under the sign-in table, and to my relief, my fingers found them. Curling my hands into a hard clutch, I concealed the weights close to my body, and began worrying how I would get them in place on the scale without making a to-do. If I were to save this woman from the

237

devil that would destroy her, I couldn't begin by embarrassing her for her sins.

In my memory, I was as smooth as Billy Graham, leading Mattie to the curtained weigh-in cubicle, and then deftly positioning the extra weights as though I did it everyday, all the while keeping up pleasant chatter with her as she stepped on to the scales. In reality, I probably gushed like a broken fire hydrant as I always do when I'm nervous and, ever clumsy, I probably clanged the weights against the beam so hard everyone in the room turned their head. But Mattie was a woman of generous spirit, and she never let on that she knew I was adapting the scales for her. Instead, she gave me a smile that lit up her handsome and intelligent face. She weighed in at 398 pounds.

I understood that vanity had not brought Mattie to Weight Watchers. A tall, big-boned country woman, her skin was weathered by decades of work in tobacco fields, and her brand of religion required her to wear her waist-length gray hair pulled back in a simple bun. Her homemade dresses hung unfitted from her shoulders like an Hawaiian muumuu, but her frocks were subdued in color, gray or navy, without flowers or pattern. No—Mattie only wanted to keep on living. Wife and daughter-in-law, mother and grandmother of a vast clan, she'd joined my group under doctor's orders.

Over the course of the next year, Mattie seesawed with her weight. Some months, she'd drop a sizable number of pounds, and I would celebrate with her, exalting her efforts in front of the class, praising her by clapping my hands and pinning milestones on her chest. The next month, she'd gain them back, and I'd go to the mourner's bench with her, imploring her to reform her ways.

Wearing cutesy sweaters and high-heeled boots that stretched to my knees, how naïve and young I must have seemed to her, and yet she never patronized me. Instead, she shared her life with me in weekly installments, offering a roadmap of what lies ahead for most of us.

Tuna fish and lettuce—I heard her saying then in her deep, husky voice—were not sufficient fuel for her battles with a capricious world, and nowhere near enough to sustain a family.

A lifetime later, I think she was telling me in her gentle way not to be so cocksure that I knew all the answers.

"Uncle so-and-so died last Friday," she'd begin "and everybody piled in for the funeral and ended up at my house and stayed till the next morning. Nothing would do them but I fix homemade biscuits and gravy and fried ham for breakfast..." and then she'd tell me about the complicated lives of her people.

The next week, her son would be in an accident or a grandchild in the hospital with pneumonia. Sometimes, the occasions would be happy ones, like weddings or births or celebrations, but these too required sustenance and nurturing from Mattie's large spirit.

One day, telling us about the vat of gravy she'd fallen in the previous week—gravy whipped up to fill a gaping hole in her family's well being—she laughed her huge laugh, and said,

"Oh Lord, let me live long enough to get bored."

Her timing was perfect. Young and old alike took her meaning, and we laughed together until we cried. Reverently. Because we understood.

In time, I lost interest in saving Ashland from its appetites, re-gained some of my own, and fell away from Weight Watchers. If Mattie ever reached her goal weight, it was long after I had left. But I've never forgotten Mattie's prayer for a little boredom in life, please.

My plate is overflowing now with happy things, scary stuff, and a long to-do list. I, too, could use a little boredom, time to go searching for a good movie or a thick novel to read. But if boredom is not mine to have in this life, thank you God that I have had the chance to meet and laugh with women like Mattie.

John Wesley Hughes

If ever a man was forgotten in the place where he was raised up, it's John Wesley Hughes, the founder of Asbury College. He was born in 1852 on a hillside farm near the village of New Columbus, only a couple of miles from where I grew up a century later, but no historical marker designates his birthplace. Today, Hughes' childhood home is so long vanished that no one living has any visual memory of it. My mother would wave her hand in the vague direction of a rolling hayfield alongside the Davis Chapel Road,[*] off to the right, or sometimes to the left, and quote Gran Hudson who'd told her the Hughes home place stood somewhere "down there." I would oblige her and crane my neck this direction and that, but I never understood where she was pointing because there was nothing to see but hay.

Davis Methodist Episcopal Chapel, where Hughes' life took an abrupt U turn during a Christmas Day revival service, is gone too. Not even a skeleton of its foundation lingers. All that remains where Hughes and God collided is a small graveyard with a few scattered markers.

In the 1880s, the Davis Chapel congregation moved over to the main road, and changed its name to the New Columbus

---

[*] On the earliest maps of the region, Davis Chapel Road is called Mountain Island Road, a long pike that began near Stamping Ground, Kentucky, in present-day Scott County, and ended at Mountain Island in present-day Owen. For most of the 19th and 20th Centuries, the lane past the old church and cemetery was called Davis Chapel Road. In the late 20th Century, the name was changed to Carr Lane, which is its designation on modern maps.

Methodist Episcopal Church (now United Methodist.) This is where I worshiped throughout my early years, where I was baptized and later married, but I never once heard John Wesley Hughes' name mentioned from that pulpit. His connection to that local congregation and to the community of his birth seems forgotten.

Hughes' Asbury College, however, is thriving. According to its website more than 20,000 living Asbury alumni surround the globe, "leading and serving" in all fifty states and in at least eighty nations, and the current enrollment is the largest in its history. Although the non-denominational school emphasizes Christian service and ideals, it's also recognized for its academic standards. *U. S. News and World Report* has ranked it among the top ten comprehensive colleges in the south for fourteen years. The Rev. John Wesley Hughes should be pleased. Committed to an educated clergy, he wrote repeatedly that he "did not advocate religion at the expense of education." He believed that education should be available to all who sought it, the poor as well as the rich.

But I'm getting ahead of the story. Hughes' people were among the earliest pioneers to settle in southern Owen County. Although he frustrates contemporary researchers by omitting first names in his autobiography, I believe his maternal grandfather was John Guill, who most think was the first settler in our Eagle Creek community. Guill fought three years in the Revolutionary War, and was at the fabled Siege of Bryan's Station near Lexington in 1781. Hughes' father, William Hughes, arrived on the Kentucky frontier as an infant in a basket slung over a horse by way of the Wilderness Road and Virginia. I mention Hughes' family origins because I'm struck by how close he was to the American Revolution—and to the frontier American Dream that anything was possible. Big, improbable dreams would define his life.

His father died "before memory began," Hughes wrote in his autobiography, and his widowed, uneducated mother eked out a meager living from the land to feed her children. It was not a likely beginning for a Greek scholar and a founder of colleges, but Hughes—after a religious conversion near as dramatic as

241

Paul's on the road to Damascus—was a man driven both by God and the American Dream.

By chance, the sixteen-year-old Hughes found himself in church on Christmas Day. He'd planned to go hunting, and then to a "social" that night, but his young friends were going to the service at Davis Chapel, so he decided to go, too. By his account, he was a wild and rambunctious lad, but an old-time revival had been sweeping through the countryside for weeks "like a prairie fire," and Hughes was seized, he writes, by the Holy Spirit. He retreated from the small church building into the woods where he wept and prayed. It would be two long days and two long nights before he was able to make peace with God.

His intense conversion experience set him on a course that would soon lead him into the ministry. With only a country grade school education, however, he felt ill equipped to preach. He writes, "As a child my literary education was wholly neglected; so my intellect long lay dormant, and was hard to awaken to the full ... possibilities. My conversion ... introduced me not only to a new realm of the spiritual world, but also to a new physical and mental world; and then I began to have a real vision of the true development of body and mind, as well as of soul—which is ... education."

With the help of a minister friend, Hughes enrolled at Kentucky Wesleyan College in 1874. "I entered ... with fear and trembling; for it was the first college I had ever seen. I was the first boy that had ever gone to college from our neighborhood."

Hughes studied there for two years before entering the Methodist Conference as an ordained, licensed minister in 1876. In 1879, he enrolled at Vanderbilt University. It's unclear to me if he received a degree from Vanderbilt, but his autobiography says he received a certificate of proficiency from the School of Moral Philosophy. By all contemporary reports, Hughes was an excellent scholar, especially of Greek and Latin.

In 1890, he fulfilled his grand vision of establishing a college that would educate "body and mind, as well as ... soul." It would be accessible to students such as he had been, frightened and poor. On September 2, The Kentucky Holiness College—later re-named Asbury—opened with eleven students and three faculty members.

Immediately, he ran into problems. For reasons not entirely clear in the scant accounts that survive, the Kentucky Methodist conference refused to accept the new school under its mantle. I think this was largely due to the Methodists' unwillingness to assist in funding a school that had little other financial backing. However, Hughes was affiliated with the Holiness Movement, a conservative theological splinter within mainstream Methodism, and that connection may have put him at a political disadvantage within the hierarchy of the Methodist Church. Thus, Asbury, though grounded in Wesleyan tradition and named for one of America's first two Methodist Bishops, became a non-denominational school from the outset, and remains so today.

Like many visionaries, Hughes was better at creating than at managing. Though his presidency had many successes, and the college enrollment grew steadily, the finances of the college remained precarious. In 1905, his board asked him to step away from the school he had breathed into being. I am left to wonder at the heartache and humiliation of this chapter of his life. He went on to found yet another college in 1906, Kingswood in Breckinridge County (which my husband's grandfather attended), but it ran aground financially, and did not survive.

He retired to Wilmore in 1915, and lived there, teaching at Asbury and preaching, until his death in 1932. With uncommon grace, he put aside his personal disappointments to celebrate Asbury and help it flourish. His contemporaries wrote that he never "exhibited any bitterness … any jealousy toward those who followed him in the presidency" but "rejoiced" in Asbury's growth.

Hughes, himself, wrote in his 1923 autobiography, "it being my college child born in poverty, mental perplexity, and soul agony, I loved it from its birth better than I loved my own life. As the days have come and gone, with many sad and broken-hearted experiences, my love has increased. My appreciation of what it has done, what it is doing, and what it promises to do in the future, is such that I am willing to lay down my life for its perpetuation."

In the twenty-first century, John Wesley's Hughes' name is a brief footnote in history, remembered by few. His dream, however, lives on in the thousands of Asbury alumni who have scattered to the four corners of the earth over the past one hundred and twenty-plus years. A few of those Asbury graduates have pastored the United Methodist congregations I've been a part of in various Kentucky communities, in Ashland, Russell, Lexington, and in my native Owen County. They've stood beside me in grief and in joy, our lives improbably connected by an impoverished, half-orphaned boy raised in the nineteenth century on an Owen County hillside not far from my own.

Aunt Georgia Belle

Aunt Georgia Belle has been on my mind this week. Actually, she's been whispering in my ear as I deck the halls this holiday season.

"Let's get out the good china," she says, "and the silver—don't forget the silver," she reminds me for the umpteenth time.

Though we shared a quaint first name, she was Ernie's aunt, not mine. But she claimed me as her own when I married into the Stamper clan over forty years ago, and set about sharing her wisdom with me.

Georgia Belle spent her life looking up, not down. Against the odds and expectations of her time and place, she became the first in her large family to go to college. She had to teach school by day on an "emergency" certificate in tiny country schools in order to afford the night and weekend classes she loved. This wasn't a quick route to a college education. It took her several decades to earn her BA degree from Georgetown College, but it was among her proudest accomplishments. In her 90s, on her deathbed, she asked every family member who stopped by her nursing home room to make sure her obituary noted she was a college graduate. And we did.

Having worked so hard for her own education, Georgia Belle gave her best effort to her students, and she expected no less of them, in and out of the classroom. "Try," she would urge them in a zillion different ways. "Try your best."

There are dozens of Georgia Belle stories worth the telling—how she went wading in the ocean for the first time when she was in her 80s, or jumped around playing games like a woman half her age at family reunions. She was funny and fun.

Butter in the Morning

But the Georgia Belle story that's haunting me this Christmas is the one about the silver candelabra. It's the right time to tell it, she whispers.

At my wedding shower, as I opened beautiful gifts from our generous family and friends, Georgia Belle leaned over and said,

"Use these things, Georgia! Whenever you entertain, get it all out, make the table beautiful—and your guests will think you're a wonderful cook regardless of how the food tastes or how little you have."

We all laughed, and so did she, but she meant what she said. It was good advice that has served me well.

She went on to tell this story on herself. Sometime in the late 40s or early 50s—anywise, in pre-credit card, penny pinching days—she saved up enough money to buy a new winter coat. Excited about her big purchase, she made a sixty-mile trip to Louisville to shop for it. But as she walked up and down Louisville's grand Fourth Street, past the beautiful windows of the big department stores like Stewarts and Kaufmans, past the jewelry stores and the specialty shops, her eye was drawn to a pair of silver candelabra. She shopped all day for a coat, and found several that would do. But her eye kept returning to the candelabra in the window. She was surprised to learn that the price tag was about the same as she'd budgeted for a good wool coat.

It was a strange fascination. Her neat little clapboard house, like most in her Owen County farm community, did not yet have indoor plumbing or central heating. Practicality was the local social norm. But at the end of the afternoon, she made her decision.

Her old coat wasn't worn out, and she could make it do for another season, she concluded. And so she came home to her white bungalow in Gratz with silver candlestick holders. Every birthday thereafter, every anniversary, every bridal shower, and sometimes for no reason at all, she'd pull out her best china and her sterling candelabra and serve whatever food she had in style.

"I never regretted the decision," she told me, "though I took a lot of teasing over it. You see, the whole extended family enjoyed the candelabra. We never had much, but the elegant candles made our occasions feel special, made us feel better about ourselves, especially when times were the roughest."

This holiday season the economic news is harsh, the worst in my lifetime. People are wisely curtailing expenditures on gifts and travel. And I'm certainly not advocating that anybody choose extravagances like silver candelabra over coats in this cold weather. In fact, I'm not advising anybody to buy anything.

But I do think it's time to pull out the best we have. If our spirits are to prevail in these hard times, we need to "try our best." Georgia Belle reminds me to look up, not down—and to light the candles.

Christmas Eve

My mother spoke to me for the last time on Christmas Eve. I suppose for some such a memory might cast a pall on Christmas forever after, but the events of that evening cause me to hold the season closer.

You have to understand that I was Mother's only child and that she synchronized the beating of her heart with my happiness. You have to understand how much effort she put into selecting the perfect Christmas gift for me each year, and for everyone else on her list, too. You have to understand how special Christmas Eve was to our family—

Julius Caesar wrote, "All Gaul is divided into three parts." My childhood world was split into only two. Half of the population, maybe less, celebrated the birth of Jesus on Christmas Eve, and the other fifty percent, maybe more, on Christmas Day.

My family belonged to the Christmas Eve believers, and like most sectarians, I grew up thinking our way was a little better. The reasons my people held with Christmas Eve have been lost to history. I suspect it had to do with impatience. All I know for sure is that roughly a hundred years ago my maternal grandparents started the tradition of a six o'clock Christmas Eve feast followed by the opening of gifts around the tree. The extended family would gather and celebrate until midnight. My mother continued her parents' ways. Even Santa co-operated, dropping my toys out in the barn no later than eight p.m. on the 24th as he hurried on to California before dawn.

Mother was not a theatrical person by nature, but she approached her annual Christmas Eve production like the opening of a Broadway show. A week or two before opening night, we'd begin work on the stage-set with a trek across the hills of our

Owen County farm to find the perfect cedar tree to cut and decorate for the living room. Of course, there is no such thing as a perfect cedar tree. Nature did not intend for them to be Christmas trees, and they defiantly grew lop-sided, too fat, too skinny, or too tall. Even when one was deemed passable, a cedar tree's branches were too weak to hold ornaments like the pines we saw in magazine pictures.

Georgia's Mother: holding baby Owen. Christmas 2004.

Mother was undaunted. With three or four cans of spray snow, hundreds of little white lights, and some plastic icicles, she'd transform our Charlie Brown tree into a Winter Wonder. Then she'd sit and stare at it night after night, whispering like a child, "Isn't it beautiful!"

The days leading up to Christmas Eve were like a sappy holiday script—except it was for real and Mother had the starring role. Christmas shopping required a rare fifty-mile trip to Lexington where she gushed over the displays of twinkling lights and the singing chipmunks in Stewart's Department Store window. Then, no matter how cold it was—in my memory it was always near zero—she would tramp up and down Main Street searching for just the right gifts. Mother was an endurance Christmas shopper, not a sprinter. Beginning at Purcell's, which stood about where Rupp Arena does today, she'd trudge to the far end of Main to Wolf Wiles, located in what is now the Grey Construction Company Building, and then back and forth a time or two until she met her self-imposed standards for the perfect gifts.

She would persuade Daddy to drive us miles over crooked roads to glimpse a live nativity scene at Bethlehem, Kentucky. She would sing holiday songs in her awful voice—the only time of year she would sing—and create singular desserts like dense blackberry-jam cake and melt-in-your-mouth marshmallow fudge.

But the climax of the show was the Christmas Eve feast. Its methodically planned menu required a cross-country jaunt to the largest supermarket around to locate hard to find items. On our return, she would begin cooking. The "old" ham was placed in a lard can and baked to tender perfection overnight. The salads—congealed, frozen, and fruit—could also be put together the day before. Christmas Eve day was spent roasting the turkey, prepping traditional vegetable dishes like mashed potatoes and new-fangled ones like steamed cauliflower with cheese sauce. And our family's secret recipe for soufflé-like dressing took a lot of attention.

At 5:30 our guests would arrive, the uncles and aunts, the cousins. At exactly six o'clock, we'd sit down in a roomful of laughter at the mahogany dining room table spread with the best dishware we owned.

250

There came a time, though, when the party passed to me and my house. Plagued by glaucoma that narrowed her field of vision, and arthritis that eventually put her in a wheelchair, Mother was no longer able to host it. But she never let go of her excitement about Christmas Eve. She continued to fret over her gifts, especially her gift to me, and ooh and ahh over the tree and outdoor light displays with childlike wonder.

In October of 2006, Mother was diagnosed with ovarian cancer. It's a silent disease, often undetected until an advanced stage, and this was Mother's situation. In November, she had surgery, and the doctor said the cancer was even more invasive than he'd expected. He warned me she had only weeks to live. And so in early December, I took her home as she asked me to do, and tried to make her comfortable.

On December 21, my Mother fell into a deep sleep, and I could not rouse her. I moved her, then, to a Hospice bed in a local hospital, and began praying she would not die on Christmas Eve.

At exactly 6 p.m. on December 24, the hour our family had sat down for Christmas dinner for a century, she woke up for the first time in three days.

"It's Christmas Eve," she said with her usual authority. "I have to get up." Euphoric, I rang for nurses to help me lift her. A pitiful-looking, but brave little tree appeared on her dresser in an instant, wrestled from a storage closet by a kind stranger. My husband found Christmas carols on his laptop computer, and turned up the volume. Then, spooning vanilla ice cream from Dixie Cups, we began our Christmas Eve dinner.

For an hour or more, we sat and talked like we always had. Lucid as ever, she asked about each of my children and my grandchildren.

One thing confused Mother. "I see a wedding going on out in the hallway, but I know that can't be happening here tonight," she said. A month later, our thirty-something daughter Shan met the man she would marry within a year's time. Perhaps it was only a morphine mirage Mother saw in the hospital corridor, but Shan, who was with us that night, does not believe it was.

After a while, Mother said she thought she should lie back down. She never woke up again. We buried her on New Year's Day.

So maybe I believe in prayer and Christmas miracles. Maybe I believe a mother's love transcends death. I do know this for certain. My mother's last Christmas gift to me was perfect.

About the Author

Georgia Green Stamper is a seventh generation Kentuckian who grew up on a tobacco farm in Owen County in the north-central area of the state. She and her husband Ernie still own the Eagle Creek land that has belonged to one member or another of her mother's people for close to a hundred and seventy years. Most of their adult working lives were spent in the Ashland area in Eastern Kentucky, however, and they now live in Lexington. They are the parents of three adult daughters and have six grandchildren.

A graduate of Transylvania University, Georgia is a former high school English and theater teacher and speech team coach. She was a published writer by the time she finished first grade when a poem she wrote appeared in the nationally circulated children's magazine *Wee Wisdom*. Despite that precocious beginning, her writing career lay dormant for decades. In 2004, however, she began writing a newspaper column "Georgia: On My Mind" for *The Owenton News-Herald.* Soon after, she became a local NPR commentator for NPR member station WUKY and has broadcast nearly one hundred of her stories on public radio. Her essays also appear regularly in *Kentucky Humanities Magazine*, and have been published in a number of literary anthologies. Her first book length collection of essays, *You Can Go Anywhere* (Wind Publications) was selected for the 2008 Carnegie Center reading series "New Books by Great Kentucky Writers." Affiliated with the Kentucky Humanities Council, she speaks frequently to groups across the state about the importance of preserving local and personal stories.

Acknowledgements

I'm not sure this book would exist had I not wandered into Leatha Kendrick's writing workshop at Lexington, Kentucky's Carnegie Center a dozen years ago. An exceptional teacher, she has become both my mentor and my editor. Her voice is ever with me as I write, and her advice, as I have struggled to organize and winnow this manuscript, has been invaluable. Thank you, Leatha, for your belief in the importance of my stories.

John Whitlock, editor of *The Owenton News-Herald*, has handled my column, the genesis of this manuscript, with respect and affection. Thank you, John, for being a cheerleader, pulling me through dry periods of discouragement, and for pushing me to jump into the blogosphere.

I am grateful for the nurturing and honest ears of my friends and fellow writers, Sherry Chandler and Stephen Rhodes. Sherry read most of these essays in the birthing process over a period of years. Steve read and critiqued the completed manuscript of *Butter in the Morning*. Thank you, Sherry, for being there time and again. Thank you, Steve, for your affirmation and for assuring me that the book was done.

I am also grateful to Ami Piccirilli, friend and fellow writer, whose response to an early version of an essay about my mother, titled "Butter in the Morning," encouraged me to begin this book. She has also given important assistance with cover art. Thank you, Ami, for everything.

I am indebted to The Kentucky Humanities Council, Dr. Virginia G. Carter, Executive Director of KHC, and Marianne Stoess, editor of *Kentucky Humanities Magazine*, for helping me scatter my stories about place and family across Kentucky. I am hopeful that our efforts have encouraged others to recover and preserve their own.

I also wish to thank George Ella Lyon who has graciously given me permission to reprint her poem "Where I'm From;" Stacy Yelton, Alan Lytle and Mike Graves at NPR member station WUKY who enabled my storytelling voice to reach a radio audience; and Linda Scott DeRosier, Gwyn Hyman Rubio, Silas House, and Joyce Dyer who encouraged my writing along the way.

Last, but not least, my husband, Ernie Stamper, has been my tireless research assistant, proofreader, photography staff of one, editorial sounding board, and the go-to reader who suffered through the first, awful draft of each essay. Thank you, Ernie, for always, always, being there for me.

Acknowledgment also is due to the publications where these essays previously were published, some in different versions and with different titles.

A version of "The Night the House Burned Down" was first published under the title "Plain Crazy" in *Motif come what may* (Motes Books) edited by Marianne Worthington.

Portions of "A Tobacco Kind of Christmas" first appeared in the essay "Where Am I From?" in *New Growth* (Jesse Stuart Foundation Press, 2007) edited by Hal Blythe & Charlie Sweet.

"The 1940 Election," "Our First Vacation" and "Go Big Blue," were re-printed in *Kentucky Humanities Magazine* after earlier versions were first published in my column "Georgia: On My Mind" in *The Owenton News-Herald*.

A longer version of "Jesse Stuart, the Bookmobile and Me" was awarded the 2007 Emma Bell Miles Award for Essay at the Lincoln Memorial University Mountain Heritage Literary Festival. An abridged version was published in 2009 in *The Owenton News-Herald* in honor of the 40th Anniversary of the Greenup County Public Library District.

A much shorter version of "Snow White" than included here was published on National Public Radio's website *This I Believe*.

"Aunt Neb," "Demi Moore Stew," "Elvis and Me," "Memorial Day," and "Narcissistic Me" were first published on my blog, "Talking to Myself," on *The Owenton News-Herald* website.

All other essays, with the exception of "A Tale of Two Autumns," "Mother," and the prologues that precede each section, were first published in my newspaper column, "Georgia: On My Mind," in *The Owenton News-Herald*.

"Baby Hudson," "Birthday Dinner," "Casual Dress," "Christmas Eve," "Class Reunion," "Classic Flu," "Coffee and Lard," "County Fair," "Dog Days of August," "First Vacation," "Funeral Fun," "Garbage Collectors," "Aunt Georgia Belle," "Mr. Stewart's Band," "1940 Election," "Rhubarb," "Taser Parties," "Technology Bullies Me," "The Garbage Collectors," and "The 1950 Thanksgiving Blizzard" also aired on NPR member station WUKY.

CPSIA information can be obtained at www.ICGtesting.com
Printed in the USA
LVOW052011240213

321475LV00002B/459/P